Microsoft Pocket Guide to Microsoft® Word 2000

Microsoft Office Application®

PUBLISHED BY
Microsoft Press
A Division of Microsoft Corporation
One Microsoft Way
Redmond, Washington 98052-6399

Library of Congress Cataloging-in-Publication Data
Nelson, Stephen L., 1959-
Microsoft Pocket Guide to Microsoft Word 2000 / Stephen L. Nelson.
p. cm.
Includes index.
ISBN 1-57231-973-9
1. Microsoft Word. 2. Word processing I. Title.
Z52.5.M52N46 1999
652.5'5369--dc21

98-44768
CIP

Printed and bound in the United States of America.

1 2 3 4 5 6 7 8 9 MLML 4 3 2 1 0 9

Distributed in Canada by ITP Nelson, a division of Thomson Canada Limited.

A CIP catalogue record for this book is available from the British Library.

Microsoft Press books are available through booksellers and distributors worldwide. For further information about international editions, contact your local Microsoft Corporation office or contact Microsoft Press International directly at fax (425) 936-7329. Visit our Web site at mspress.microsoft.com.

Acquisitions Editor: Susanne M. Forderer
Project Editor: Anne Taussig

Microsoft Pocket Guide to Microsoft® Word 2000

Microsoft Office Application®

Stephen L. Nelson

Microsoft® Press

The Microsoft Pocket Guide to Microsoft Word 2000 *is divided into five sections. These sections are designed to help you find the information you need quickly.*

1 Environment

Terms and ideas you'll want to know to get the most out of Microsoft Word. All the basic parts of Word are shown and explained. The emphasis here is on quick answers, but many topics are cross-referenced so that you can find out more if you want to.

Diagrams of key components, with quick definitions, cross-referenced to more complete information.

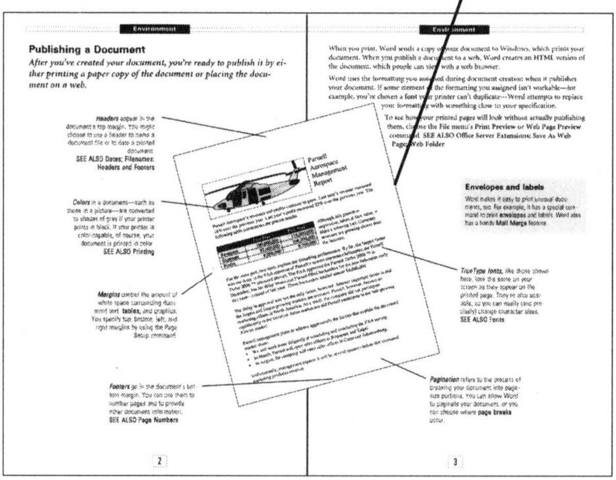

Tips

Watch for these as you use this Pocket Guide. They'll point out helpful hints and let you know what to watch for.

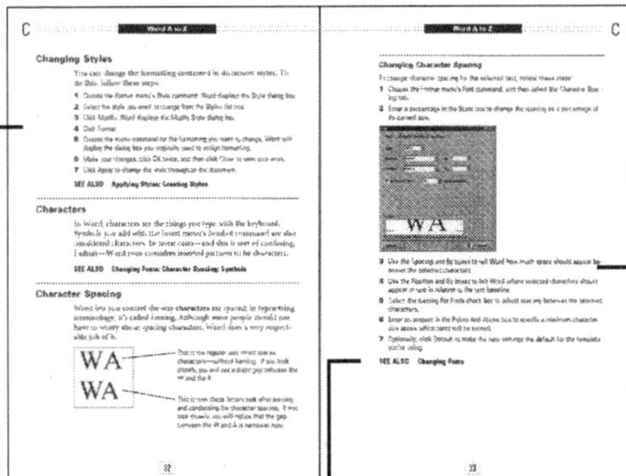

Definitions of key concepts and terms, and examples showing you why you should know them.
Step-by-step guides to performing most Internet tasks.
Cross-references to related topics.

Introduction

This Pocket Guide provides quick, practical answers to just about any question you have about Microsoft Word 2000. To acquaint yourself with this convenient and easy-to-use book, take two minutes now and read the Introduction. It explains how this unusual little book works.

What Is a Pocket Guide?

One of the problems with larger books about computers is, quite frankly, their size. With large books, you must typically sift through pages of information to find that one piece of information you need. Not only that, you have to contend with their physical size. It's rarely enjoyable and often not practical to lug around a thousand-page book if you're working both at home and at the office, or if you're on the road with your laptop.

The *Microsoft Pocket Guide to Microsoft Word 2000* addresses both "size" problems of the larger computer books. Most obvious, of course, is the fact that this book is smaller. So it's easier to carry the book around wherever you go.

But this Pocket Guide also addresses the problem of wading through a large book to find the piece of information you need. It does so in a variety of ways. For starters, this Pocket Guide organizes its information by using an A-to-Z scheme—just like a dictionary or an encyclopedia does. This Pocket Guide supplies visual indexes in its Environment section, so you can find help even if you don't know how to describe what it is you're looking for. Finally, this Pocket Guide also uses a rich cross-referencing scheme that points you to related topics.

For new users, the Pocket Guide provides the essential information necessary to start using Word. For experienced users, the Pocket Guide provides concise, easy-to-find descriptions of Word tasks, terms, and techniques.

When You Have a Question

Let me explain how to find the information you need. If Word is new to you, flip first to the Environment section, which is a visual index. Find the picture that shows what you want to do or the task you have a question about. For example, if you want to know how to write a report, flip to pages 4 and 5, which show you how to create documents—such as reports—in Word.

Next read the captions that describe the parts of the picture. Say, for example, that you want to include a **table** in the report. The picture on pages 4 and 5 includes a caption that describes how to add tables to documents.

You'll notice that some captions use **boldface** terms or are followed by additional boldface terms. These refer to entries in the second section, Word A to Z, and provide more information related to the caption's contents.

Word A to Z is a dictionary of more than 200 entries that define terms and describe tasks. (After you've worked with Word a little or if you're already an experienced user, you'll often be able to turn directly to that section.) So if you have just read an entry that talks about AutoFormatting your report, you'll see the term **AutoFormat** in boldface, indicating a cross-reference. If you want to know how to format your report automatically, turn to the AutoFormat entry in Word A to Z.

When an entry in Word A to Z appears as a term within another entry, I'll often **boldface** it the first time it appears in that entry. For example, as part of describing what an **object** is, I might tell you that you use objects to drag and drop a Microsoft Excel spreadsheet into a document. In this case, the term **drag-and-drop** appears in bold letters—alerting you to the presence of another entry explaining this term. If you don't understand the term or want to do some brushing up, you can flip to the entry for more information.

When You Have a Problem

The third section, Troubleshooting, describes problems that new and casual users of Word often encounter. Following each problem description, I list one or more solutions you can employ to fix the problem.

When You Wonder About a Command

The Quick Reference at the end of the Pocket Guide describes the Word menu commands and toolbar buttons. If you want to know what a specific command or button does, turn to the Quick Reference. Don't forget about the Index, either. You can look there to find all references to any single topic in this book.

Conventions Used Here

I have developed a few conventions to make using this book easier for you. Rather than use wordy phrases such as "Activate the File menu and then choose the Print command" to describe how you choose a menu command, I'm just going to say, "Choose the File menu's Print command."

Here's another convention: To make dialog box button and box labels stand out, I've capitalized the initial letter of each word in the label. I think this technique makes it easier to understand an instruction such as "Select the Print To File check box." With this scheme, it's easier to see, for example, that "Print To File" is a label.

One final point: In general, I try to tell you the easiest, most direct way to get things done. For example, I'll often suggest you use **shortcut menu** commands or toolbar buttons instead of conventional menu commands. I also assume you know how to select menu commands, windows, and dialog box elements by using either the mouse or the keyboard.

Environment

Need to get oriented? Then the Environment is the place to start. It defines the key terms you'll need to know and the core ideas you should understand as you begin exploring Microsoft Word 2000.

The Word Program Window

When you start Microsoft Word, Windows displays the Word program window. In the program window, Word provides an empty, ready-to-use document window.

The ***menu bar*** lists the commands you choose to create, print, and save your documents.

SEE ALSO Opening New Documents; Printing; Saving Documents

The ***title bar*** identifies the application—Microsoft Word—and the names of the author and document.

SEE ALSO Documents

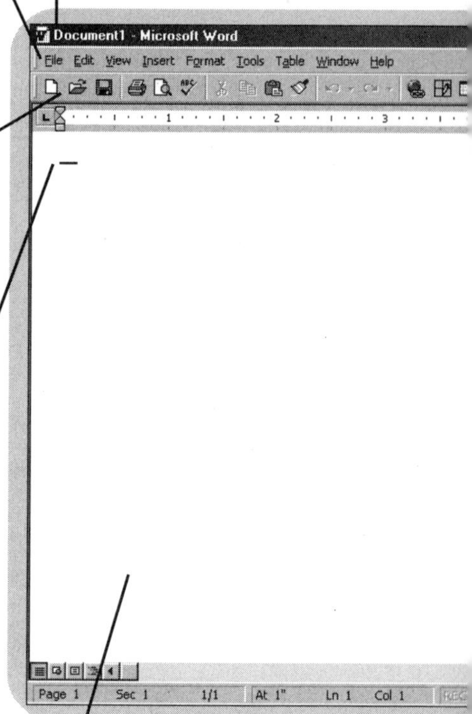

The ***toolbar*** provides clickable buttons and boxes you can use to aid in creating a document and editing its contents.

SEE ALSO Editing Tables; Editing Text; Fonts; Formatting

The ***insertion point*** shows where Word will place the next character you type. You can move the insertion point by moving the mouse and then clicking.

The ***document window*** shows the text you've typed and anything else you've added to your document—such as graphics or **tables.**

Microsoft Word is, essentially, a document-creation tool. That sounds complicated, but you've almost certainly been creating **documents** for years: personal letters, school reports, and business memos, to name a few.

Simple documents may include only text. Using Word, however, you can create complex documents that include text, pictures, and **tables.**

Word also provides tools for preparing elements—**indexes, tables of contents,** and **footnotes**—common to formal and lengthy documents. And Word includes writing and editing tools—such as a **spelling** checker, a **thesaurus** (or synonym-antonym finder), and a **grammar checker**. What's more, with Word you can create World Wide Web pages and make **hyperlinks.**

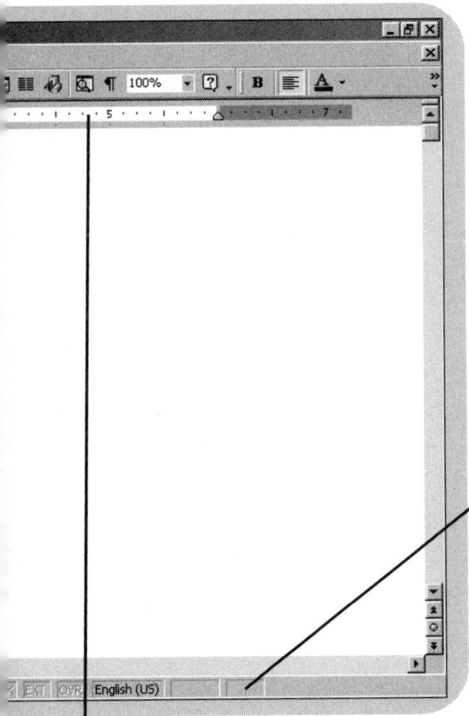

Word and Windows

You will want to learn the basics of the Microsoft Windows operating environment before you start learning and working with Microsoft Word. Although you don't need to become an expert, you should know how to choose commands from menus and work with dialog box elements: boxes, buttons, and lists. If you don't possess this core knowledge, refer to the first few chapters of your Windows documentation.

The ***status bar*** describes your document and the background activities of Word—such as automatic document saving and printing.
SEE ALSO Saving Documents

The ***ruler*** shows your page **margins** and indents. By dragging the mouse, you can change margins and indents.
SEE ALSO Indentation and Alignment

Creating a Document

Creating a document in Word consists of two interrelated activities: collecting the information you want in the document and describing how that information should be displayed.

Pictures can be placed in the document by using the Insert menu's Picture command. (Word comes with a **clip art** gallery of hundreds of images.)

Paragraph formatting options let you change line spacing and indentations.
SEE ALSO Indentation and Alignment; Paragraph and Line Spacing

Tables efficiently organize information into columns and rows. You can even write **formulas** that calculate amounts.

Views are different ways of looking at a document. You choose whether you want to see a document as a long **column** of text (Normal or Web Layout), as pages of text (Print Layout, shown here), or as an **outline** of your headings.

Document text is entered by typing at the keyboard, a process much the same as typing on a typewriter.
SEE ALSO Entering Text; Word Wrap

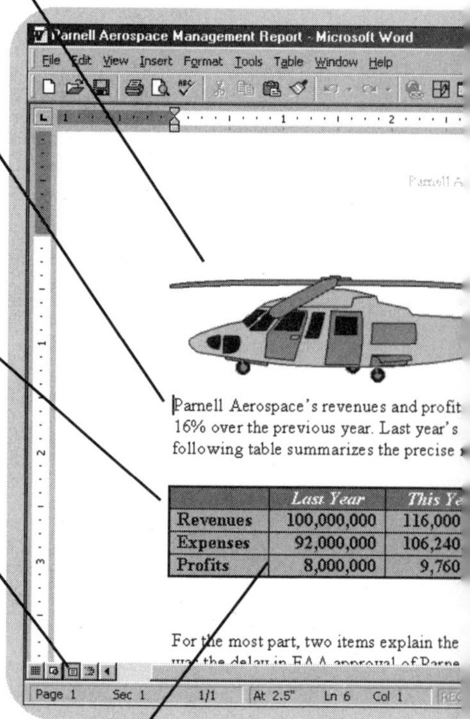

Borders and ***shading*** can be added to increase readability and visual interest.

Document creation starts with **entering text** in the **document window.** Many documents—perhaps most—will contain only text. But you can add other elements—such as pictures, **tables,** and special **symbols.**

After you've finished entering a document's text, you'll often want to adjust the suggested **formatting** that Word applies to your documents. You may want to change paragraph formatting by adjusting line spacing or indentation. You may want to change the character formatting by using another **font,** a different point size, or a special character style, such as **bold** or *italic.*

SEE ALSO **Bold Characters; Indentation and Alignment; Italic Characters; Paragraph and Line Spacing**

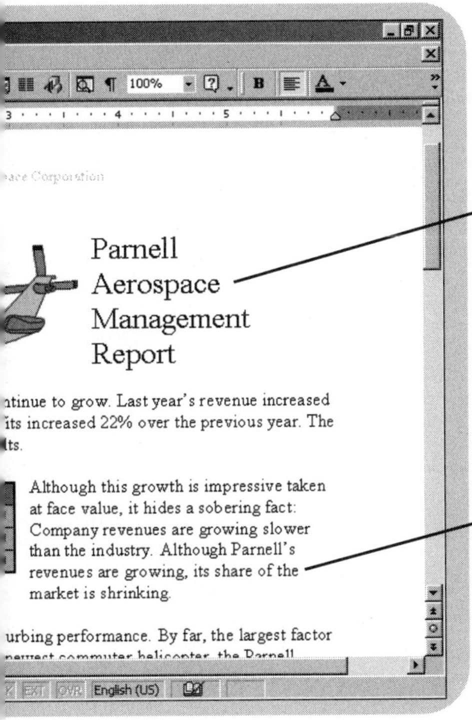

Font formatting options let you change character **fonts, styles,** and **point** sizes. Your printed document includes this **formatting**.

Word wrap is automatic. Word moves the **insertion point** and text to the next line when you've filled a line to its maximum length.

Publishing a Document

After you've created your document, you're ready to publish it by either printing a paper copy of the document or placing the document on a web.

Headers appear in the document's top margin. You might choose to use a header to name a document file or to **date** a printed document. **SEE ALSO Filenames; Headers and Footers**

Colors in a document—such as those in a picture—are converted to shades of gray if your printer **prints** in black. If your printer is color-capable, of course, your document is printed in color.

Margins control the amount of white space surrounding document text, **tables,** and graphics. You specify top, bottom, left, and right margins by using the Page Setup command.

Footers go in the document's bottom margin. You can use them to number pages and to provide other document information. **SEE ALSO Page Numbers**

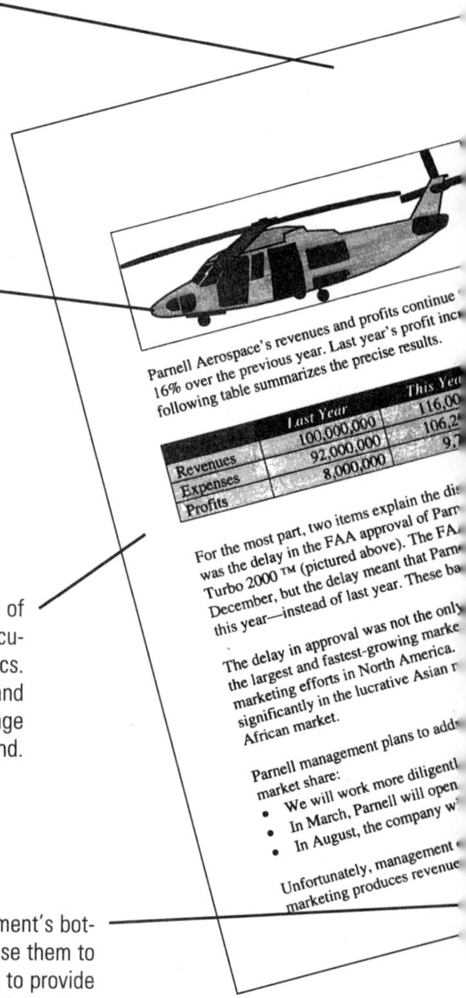

When you print, Word sends a copy of your document to Windows, which prints your document. When you publish a document to a web, Word creates an **HTML** version of the document, which people can view with a web browser.

Word uses the formatting you assigned during document creation when it publishes your document. If some element of the formatting you assigned isn't workable—for example, you've chosen a **font** your printer can't duplicate—Word attempts to replace your formatting with something close to your specification.

To see how your printed pages will look without actually publishing them, choose the File menu's **Print Preview** or **Web Page Preview** command.

SEE ALSO **Office Server Extensions; Saving Web Pages; Web Folder**

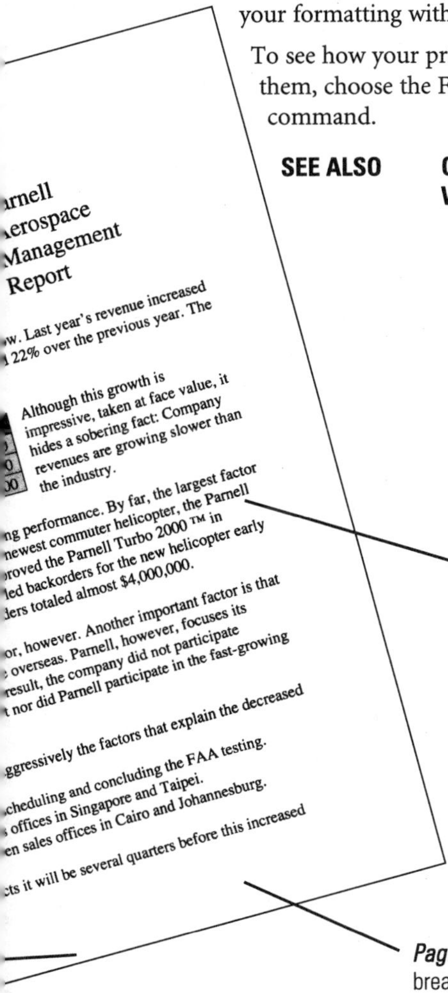

Envelopes and labels

Word makes it easy to print unusual documents, too. For example, it has a special command to print **envelopes** and labels. Word also has a handy **Mail Merge** feature.

TrueType fonts, like those shown here, look the same on your screen as they appear on the printed page. They're also scalable, so you can easily (and precisely) change character sizes.
SEE ALSO Fonts

Pagination refers to the process of breaking your document into page-size portions. You can allow Word to paginate your document, or you can choose where **page breaks** occur.

Word

A to Z

When you have a question, you want a quick, easy answer. Word A to Z, which starts on the next page, should provide just these sorts of answers. It lists in alphabetic order the tools, terms, and techniques you'll need to know.

Active and Inactive Windows

The active **document window** is the one you see in the Word **program window**. Any Word commands you choose affect the document in the active document window.

The active program window—such as the Word program window—is the one that appears in front of any other program windows on your screen. (That window is called the foreground. The inactive program windows, if inactive programs are running, appear in the background.)

Opening Program Windows

You can open a different program window by clicking the window or by clicking its button on the Taskbar.

Opening Document Windows

You can open a different document window by clicking the window, clicking its button on the Taskbar, or choosing the Window menu command that names the window.

Active Document

The active **document** is the one you can see in the Word **program window**. That document is also the one that chosen commands act on.

Changing the active document

You can flip-flop between open documents—if you have more than one open—by pressing Alt Tab, or by choosing one of the numbered menu commands from the Window menu. Each numbered command names a different document window.

Adaptability

Word customizes its menus so that they supply only the commands you choose and its toolbars so that they provide only the tools you use. This adaptability makes it easier for you to find the menu commands and toolbar buttons you regularly use.

You still have access to all Word's features even with its adaptability, however. If you point to the double-arrow at the bottom of a menu or linger on a menu without choosing a command, Word displays its long menus, which supply all your commands. If you click the double arrow toolbar button, you display an extended set of toolbar buttons.

SEE ALSO Personal Menus and Toolbars

Adding Document Pictures

You can easily add pictures to a document as long as a file is storing the picture on disk. Note too that Word comes with hundreds of clip art pictures stored in the Clipart folder.

Inserting Pictures

1 Move the insertion point to where the picture should be placed.

2 Choose the Insert menu's Picture command.

3 Choose the submenu's Clip Art command.

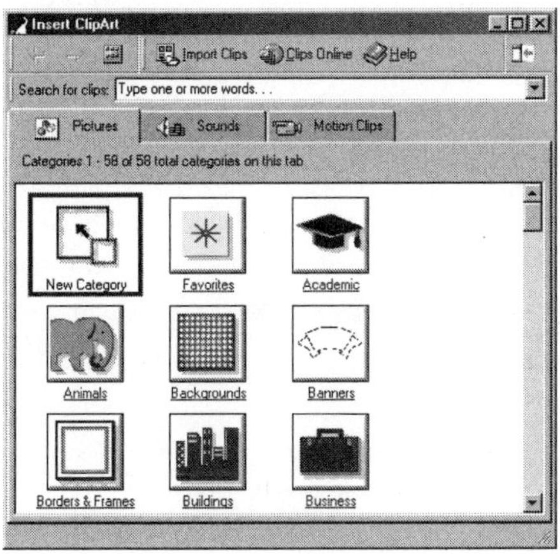

4 Click the Pictures, Sounds, or Motion Clips tab.

5 Scroll to see the image, sound, or video you want. Click it, and click the Insert Clip icon.

continues

Adding Document Pictures *(continued)*

Copying Pictures

If a picture already exists in a document, you can copy it to a new location. To do this, select the picture, choose the Edit menu's Copy command, reposition the insertion point, and then choose the Edit menu's Paste command.

SEE ALSO **Charts; Drag-and-Drop; Drawing; Moving Pictures; Resizing Pictures; Selecting; WordArt**

Alignment SEE Indentation and Alignment

Annotations SEE Comments

Application Window

The application window is the rectangle in which an application such as Word displays its menu bar, **toolbars**, and any open **document windows**. This book refers to application windows as program windows because the window appears after you start a program.

Applying Styles

To apply a **style** to the current selection, click the Style toolbar button down-arrow to open the Style box and select a style.

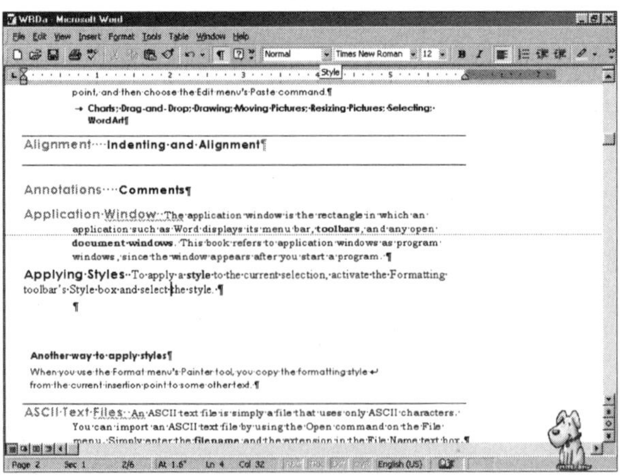

Another way to apply styles

When you use the Personal toolbar's Format Painter tool, you copy the formatting style from the current insertion point to some other text.

ASCII Text Files

An ASCII text file is simply a file that uses only ASCII characters. You can import an ASCII text file by using the File menu's Open command. Simply enter the **filename** and the extension in the File Name text box.

Sharing data among programs

Word will open, or import, a text file. Many programs—spreadsheets, databases, and accounting programs, among others—produce text files. Note, then, that you can share data among programs by moving the data as a text file—particularly as a text file that contains only ASCII characters.

SEE ALSO Importing Documents

AutoComplete

People type many phrases frequently: the current date; letter salutations and closings; and notices like Attn, Confidential, and Via Overnight Mail. Word knows about many commonly typed phrases. When you start typing them, a tip appears above the insertion point and displays the entire phrase Word thinks that you want to type. To let the Word AutoComplete feature finish typing the phrase for you, press Enter. If the AutoComplete guess isn't correct, just ignore it and keep typing. The tip disappears.

continues

AutoComplete *(continued)*

To Turn AutoComplete on or off, follow these steps:

1. Choose the Insert menu's AutoText command, and then choose the submenu's AutoText command.
2. In the dialog box, click the AutoText tab.

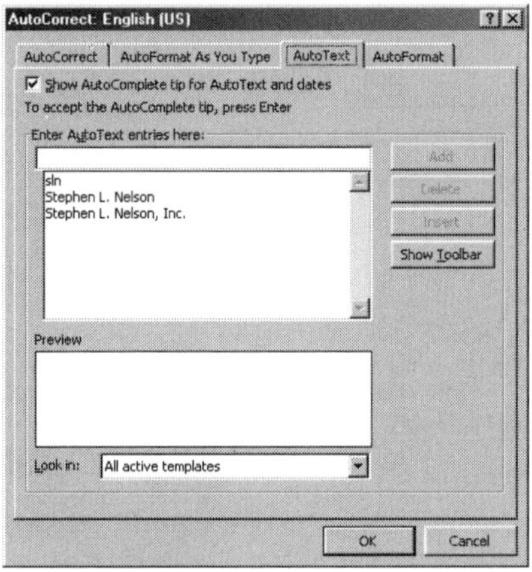

3. Select the Show AutoComplete Tip For AutoText And Dates check box to turn AutoComplete on. Or click to clear this box and turn AutoComplete off.

Expanding AutoComplete's power

You can tell AutoComplete to finish your personal collection of most frequently typed phrases by adding them as AutoText entries and making sure that AutoComplete is turned on.

AutoCorrect

AutoCorrect seeks out and corrects many types of common errors as you work, including errors in spelling, nonstandard capitalization, and more. For instance, if you misspell the word *the* as *teh,* AutoCorrect fixes your mistake. If you find AutoCorrect making changes that aren't corrections, however, you can fine-tune the **AutoCorrect Options**.

AutoCorrect Options

AutoCorrect works well as the Word Setup program installs it, but you can fine-tune its operation. To change the way AutoCorrect works, follow these steps:

1. Choose the Tools menu's AutoCorrect command.
2. Select check boxes in the AutoCorrect dialog box for the corrections you want Word to make.

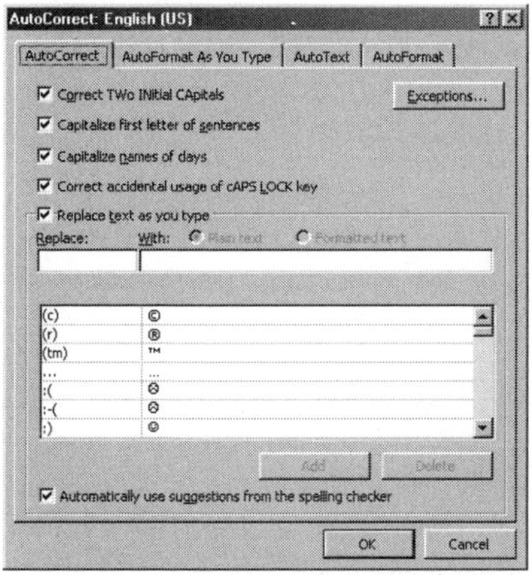

3. Select the Replace Text As You Type check box to have Word fix spelling mistakes as you make them. (I recommend using this feature.)
4. To augment Word's list of commonly misspelled words, type the misspelling in the Replace text box and then type the correct spelling in the With text box.
5. Click Add to add the misspelled word/correctly spelled word combination to the list box.
6. To specify words you don't want AutoCorrect to change according to the "normal" rules of capitalization, just click Exceptions, type the words in the appropriate box on either the First Letter tab or Initial Caps tab, and then click Add. Word will then recognize your preferred versions of these words as valid.

Additional AutoCorrect features

If you select the Correct Accidental Usage Of Caps Lock Key option, Word will automatically insert the correctly capitalized or lowercase version of a word you've typed with the Caps Lock key inadvertently turned on, and then it will turn off the Caps Lock key for you. You can also use the Replace and With boxes to replace specified text with symbols of your choosing. (This way, you don't have to bother navigating through menus and dialog box tabs every time you want to insert a symbol that's not on the keyboard.) If you ask it to, AutoCorrect will even replace text or symbols you use repeatedly with something other than text or symbols, such as a logo.

AutoFormat

If you want, you can tell Word to **format** your **document** for you automatically. To do this, choose the Format menu's AutoFormat command. Word looks through your document and then formats it by applying a set of standard **styles**.

If you choose AutoFormat And Review Each Change, Word gives you the chance to review and either accept or reject the changes AutoFormat has made—either in total or individually (by clicking Review Changes and using the forward and backward Find buttons)—and the chance to apply custom styles from the Style Gallery.

You'll also want to check out the AutoFormat As You Type option. Choose the Tools menu's AutoCorrect command, and click the AutoFormat As You Type tab. Select the check boxes next to the items you want to turn on (checked) or off (cleared).

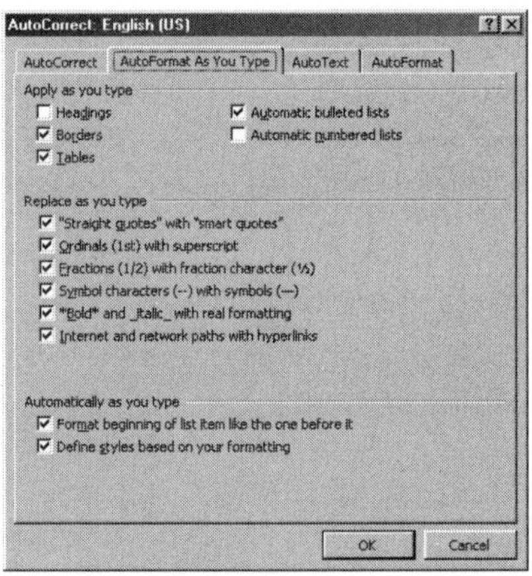

This setting does exactly what its name suggests; just select in its groups of options whatever check boxes you want. As soon as you close the Options dialog box and begin typing your document, Word will start applying the formatting, making the adjustments, and replacing the characters you specified.

Automatic Grammar Checking

Word can check the grammar of your documents automatically. If Word sees a phrase or sentence that looks erroneous, it underlines the word with a wavy green line. If you right-click the word, Word displays a shortcut menu that lists suggested edits (if Word can guess how the phrase or sentence should be rewritten) and commands you can use to tell Word that the phrase or sentence is written correctly.

You can exert quite a bit of control over the way Word checks grammar. To do this, choose the Tools menu's Spelling And Grammar command. Then click Options in the Spelling And Grammar dialog box. Select Grammar check boxes to describe how and when you want grammar checked. Select an option from the Writing Style drop-down list box to indicate the grammar standard to which you want to hold your document. You can also click Settings to display a list box that lets you select which grammar rules Word applies in its grammar checking.

SEE ALSO **Automatic Spell Checking; Readability**

Automatic Spell Checking

Word spell-checks your documents automatically. If it sees a word that looks misspelled, it underlines the word with a wavy red line.

Using Automatic Spell Checking

If you right-click the word, Word displays a shortcut menu that lists suggested spellings (if Word can guess what you've tried to spell) and commands you can use to tell Word that the word is spelled correctly. If the Word shortcut menu lists the word you wanted to spell, select it. If not, choose the Spelling command. The Spelling dialog box appears. To use the Spelling dialog box, follow the steps on the next page:

continues

Automatic Spell Checking *(continued)*

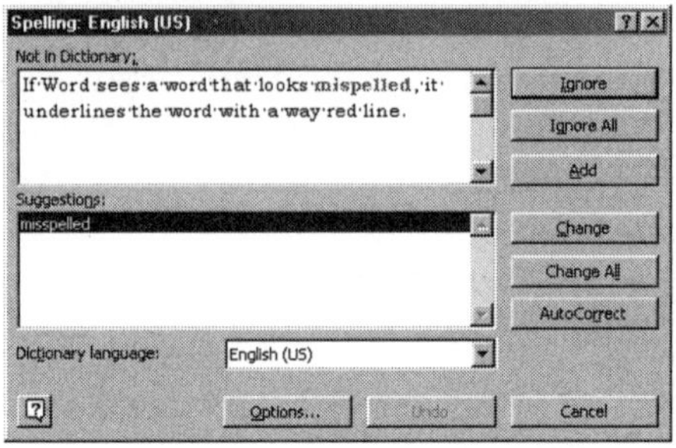

1. Type the correct spelling in the Not In Dictionary box, or select the word you want in the Suggestions list, if you see it there, and click Change. Or if you want to leave the word spelled as it is, click either Ignore or Ignore All.
2. If you want to fix all subsequent occurrences of the word, click Change All.
3. If Word has incorrectly identified a word as misspelled and you want to add the word to the Word spelling dictionary, click Add.

Fine-Tuning Automatic Spell Checking

As with automatic grammar checking, you can control the way Word checks spelling. To do this, follow these steps:

1. Choose the Tools menu's Options command.
2. Click the Spelling & Grammar tab.
3. Select Spelling check boxes to specify how and when Word should check spelling. For example, if you want Word to check spelling as you type, select the Check Spelling As You Type check box.

Edit your dictionary

You can edit your custom dictionary by selecting it, clicking the Dictionaries button, and then clicking Edit.

AutoRecover

You can tell Word that it should automatically save your documents on a regular basis. To turn on the AutoRecover feature, follow these steps:

1. Choose the Tools menu's Options command.
2. Click the Save tab.

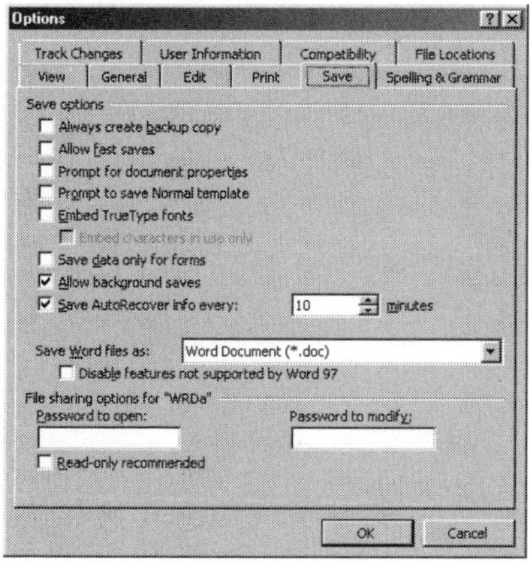

3. Select the Save AutoRecover Info Every check box to turn on Word's automatic file-recovery feature.
4. Specify how often the document file should be saved for recovery. Word saves the document in the same location and with the same filename.

SEE ALSO Saving Documents

AutoSummarize

This handy, new feature automatically creates a summary of key points in the active document. Choose the Tools menu's AutoSummarize command to tell Word to highlight key points in your document, build an executive summary or abstract at its head, or create a summary in a separate document. To use AutoSummarize, follow the steps on the next page:

continues

AutoSummarize *(continued)*

1 Choose the Tools menu's AutoSummarize command.

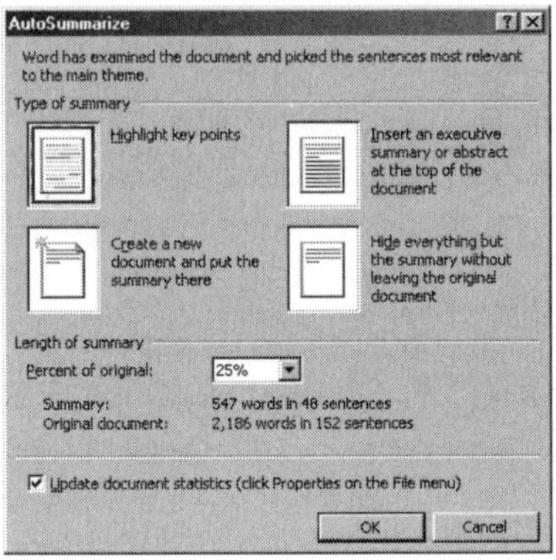

2 In the Type of Summary area, select the kind of summary you want.

3 Select a percentage from the Percent Of Original drop-down list box to tell Word how long to make the summary in terms of percentage of the original document.

4 Select the Update Document Statistics check box to update document statistics (the ones listed in the File menu's Properties dialog box) when summarizing.

5 Click OK.

If you chose to highlight key points in the document or to hide everything except the summary, the AutoSummarize toolbar appears along with the completed summary. Click Highlight/Show Only Summary to switch between viewing the whole document with key points highlighted and the summary only. Click Close on the AutoSummarize toolbar to return to a normal view of your document without the summary.

AutoText

You can use AutoText to automate the entry of a word or phrase you type repeatedly. For example, if you have to type a lengthy product name again and again—particularly if it's one that's easy to misspell—you can create an AutoText entry for the text. After you create an AutoText entry, all you need to do is begin typing the product name. As soon as Word recognizes what you're doing, it completes the text. To accept the completed text, press Enter.

Creating an AutoText Entry

To create an AutoText entry, enter the word or phrase in a document. Then select the phrase, and press Alt+F3. (Press these two keys simultaneously.) Word displays the Create AutoText dialog box.

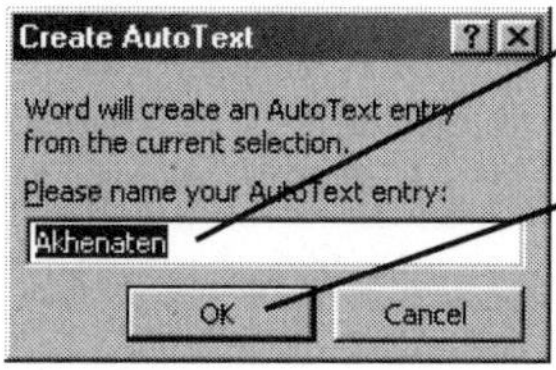

1 Enter the portion of text you want entered automatically.

2 Click OK.

With this AutoText entry, you can enter the word *Akhenaten* by simply typing the first part of the word and then pressing Enter when the tip box appears and shows the entire word.

Deleting an AutoText Entry

To delete an AutoText entry, choose the Insert menu's AutoText command and then choose the submenu's AutoText command. Select in the list box the entry to be deleted, and click Delete. Click OK to close the dialog box.

Bold Characters

You can make characters **bold** by selecting them and then pressing Ctrl+B or by clicking the Bold toolbar button. You can also choose the Format menu's Font command. To remove bold formatting, press Ctrl+B or click the Bold toolbar button again.

SEE ALSO Changing Fonts

Bookmarks

Bookmarks flag lines in a document so that you can quickly move there.

When you add a bookmark, you can quickly move to the place it marks by choosing the Insert menu's Bookmark command, clicking the bookmark, and then clicking **Go To.**

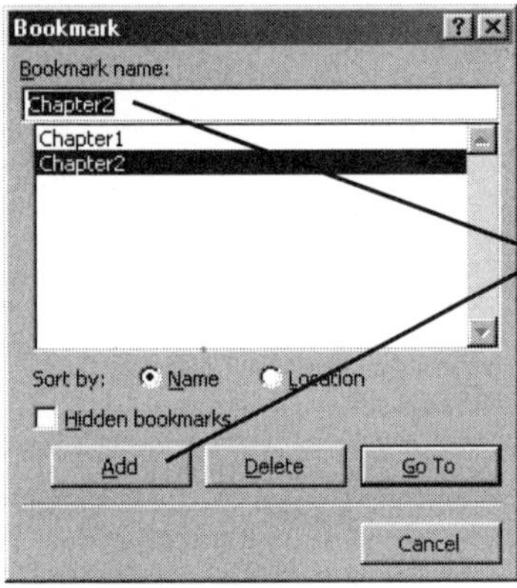

First place the insertion point where you want the bookmark.

Then choose the Insert menu's Bookmark command.

When Word displays the Bookmark dialog box, create a new bookmark by typing its name and then clicking Add.

Note that bookmark names cannot have spaces in them.

SEE ALSO Go To

Borders

You can add borders to **paragraphs** and **tables.**

SEE ALSO Page Borders; Paragraph Borders

Bulleted Lists

Bulleted lists let you neatly organize short lists of items, including **paragraphs**, as shown in the following document fragment.

Goals for Coming Year:

- Budget regular training time for team members
- Boost speed by another ten percent
- Eliminate overtime

Creating a Bulleted List

In a bulleted list, each paragraph is preceded by a bullet point. The simplest way to add bullets is by selecting the paragraphs and then clicking the Bullet toolbar button.

Another way to add bullets is by selecting the paragraph and then choosing the Format menu's Bullets And Numbering command. When Word displays the Bullets And Numbering dialog box, follow these steps:

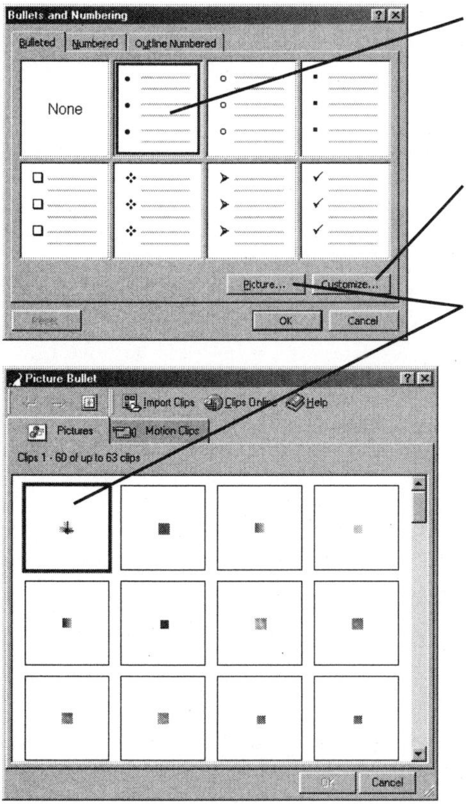

1 If you want to create a bulleted list that looks like one of the examples shown in the dialog box, click one of the bulleted list examples.

2 Optionally, click Customize, and then specify bullet character, bullet position, and text position.

3 If you want to create a bulleted list that uses pictures, click Picture. Then when Word displays the Picture Bullet dialog box, select the picture bullet you want to use.

4 Click OK.

continues

Bulleted Lists *(continued)*

Adding Bulleted List Entries

To add entries to a bulleted list, place the **insertion point** at the end of an existing entry, press Enter, and type your new bullet entry.

Removing Bulleted List Entries

To remove an entry from a bulleted list, select it and press Delete. To remove just the bullet, select the bulleted list and click the Bullet toolbar button. Or select the entry, choose the Format menu's Bullets And Numbering command, and click None.

Bullets, AutoCorrect, and AutoFormat

If you try to create your own bulleted list by using keyboard characters—asterisks, for example—Word will automatically replace your bogus bullets, if you let it. To make sure that this feature is turned on, choose the Tools menu's AutoCorrect command and click the AutoFormat As You Type tab. Make sure that the Automatic Bulleted Lists check box is selected. If you want to turn keyboard-character bullets into real ones after they're already typed, note too that you can select the list, choose the Format menu's **AutoFormat** command, and click OK.

SEE ALSO Numbered Lists

Cells

Cells are the row-column intersections, or boxes, in **tables**. You can enter text, numbers, and even **formulas** in these cells.

Cells have names. These names combine the table column letter and the table row number. The first column is A, the second is B, and so on. The first row is 1, the second is 2, and so on. The leftmost, topmost cell, therefore, is A1.

SEE ALSO Creating Tables

Changing Fonts

To change the **font** used for the selected text, choose the Format menu's Font command. When Word displays the Font dialog box, follow these steps:

1 Select a font from the Font list box. Word identifies printer fonts with the printer icon and TrueType fonts with the TrueType logo in the Fonts list on the Formatting toolbar.

2 Indicate whether you want regular (roman) characters, bold characters, italic characters, or bold italic characters by using the Font Style list box.

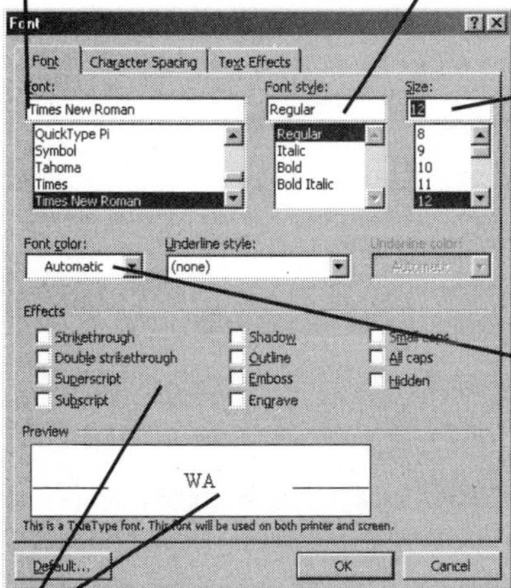

3 Select a point size from the Size list box. (One point equals 1/72 inch.)

4 Add color using the Color drop-down list box. (Auto—automatic—usually means black.)

5 If appropriate, apply one or more special effects (for example, superscript or subscript) by selecting Effects check boxes. Word has some great font effects—shadow, outline, emboss, engrave—go ahead and experiment. You can see the effect in the Preview box.

SEE ALSO Character Spacing; Font Animation; Points and Point Size

Changing Styles

You can change the formatting contained in document **styles.** To do this, follow these steps:

1. Choose the Format menu's Style command. Word displays the Style dialog box.
2. Select the style you want to change from the Styles list box.
3. Click Modify. Word displays the Modify Style dialog box.
4. Click Format.
5. Choose the menu command for the formatting you want to change. Word will display the dialog box you originally used to assign formatting.
6. Make your changes, click OK twice, and then click Close to save your work.
7. Click Apply to change the style throughout the document.

SEE ALSO Applying Styles; Creating Styles

Characters

In Word, characters are the things you type with the keyboard. Symbols you add with the Insert menu's Symbol command are also considered characters. In some cases—and this is sort of confusing, I admit—Word even considers inserted pictures to be characters.

SEE ALSO Changing Fonts; Character Spacing; Symbols

Character Spacing

Word lets you control the way **characters** are spaced; in typesetting terminology, it's called *kerning*. Although most people should not have to worry about spacing characters, Word does a very respectable job of it.

This is the regular way Word spaces characters—without kerning. If you look closely, you will see a slight gap between the W and the A.

This is how these letters look after kerning and condensing the character spacing. If you look closely, you will notice that the gap between the W and A is narrower now.

Changing Character Spacing

To change character spacing for the selected text, follow these steps:

1 Choose the Format menu's Font command, and then click the Character Spacing tab.

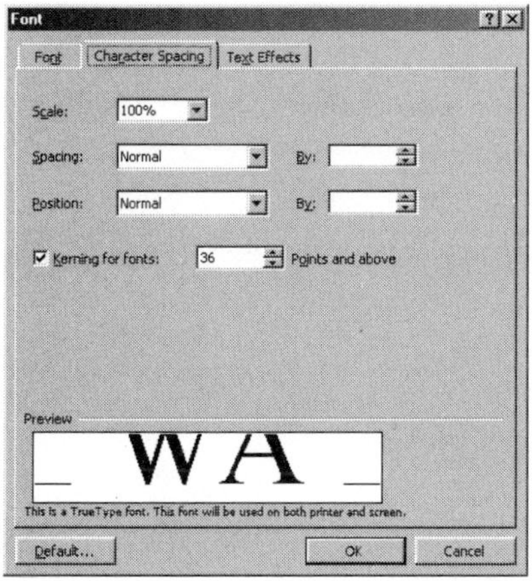

2 Enter a percentage in the Scale box to change the spacing as a percentage of its current size.

3 Use the Spacing and By boxes to tell Word how much space should appear between the selected characters.

4 Use the Position and By boxes to tell Word where selected characters should appear in text in relation to the text baseline.

5 Select the Kerning For Fonts check box to adjust spacing between the selected characters.

6 Enter an amount in the Points And Above box to specify a minimum character size above which fonts will be kerned.

7 Optionally, click Default to make the new settings the default for the template you're using.

SEE ALSO Changing Fonts

Charts

A chart, or **graph**, is a visual depiction of numeric data. Pie charts are one example; line graphs are another. In Word, you can create these pictures-worth-a-thousand-words with the Microsoft Graph application. Microsoft Graph comes with Word.

Note that if you've worked with the Microsoft **Excel** charting feature, you'll probably find that using Microsoft Graph is quite straightforward. Microsoft Graph works almost exactly like the Excel charting feature.

SEE ALSO Embedding and Linking Existing Objects; Graphs

Clip Art

Clip art refers to the graphics images you can paste into documents. Word comes with hundreds of clip art images, stored as files in the Clipart folder. If you've upgraded from a previous version of Word, you probably also have a Clipart subfolder that stores a bunch more clip art files.

SEE ALSO Adding Document Pictures

ClipArt Gallery SEE Adding Document Pictures

Clipboard

When you copy or cut a selection from a Word document, Word copies your selection from the document to the Windows Clipboard, a temporary storage area. When you later paste the selection, Word pastes the selection from the Clipboard back to the document. If you copy or cut more than one selection to the Clipboard, Windows displays the Clipboard toolbar. It shows how many items you've stored on the Clipboard. (If you don't see the Clipboard toolbar, choose the View menu's Toolbars command and then choose the submenu's Clipboard command.)

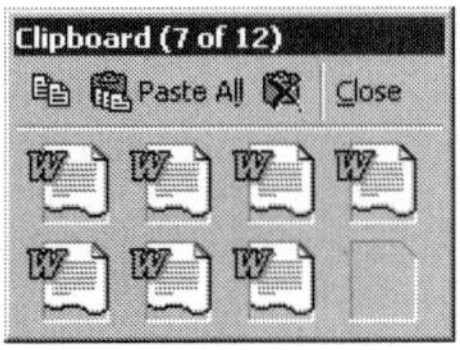

If you choose the Edit menu's Paste command or click the Paste toolbar button, the most recent addition to the Clipboard gets pasted back into your document. You can use the Clipboard window to paste an item other than the most recent Clipboard addition. To do this, click the picture representing the selection you want to paste. If you don't know which Clipboard picture represents which copied or cut selection, point to the picture so that Windows will display a pop-up box describing the Clipboard contents. Two final, quick notes about the Clipboard window: you can click Paste All to paste everything you've stored on the Clipboard into the active document—probably a Word document—and you can click Clear Clipboard in the Clipboard window to erase the contents of the Clipboard.

SEE ALSO Copying

Closing Documents

You close **documents** so they don't consume memory and so they don't clutter your screen.

Closing a Single Document

To close a single document, either click its Close button (the one in the upper right corner with an X on it) or make sure that the document is active and then choose the File menu's Close command. Be careful not to confuse a document's Close button with the application's Close button.

Closing All Open Documents

To close all open **document windows** at one time, hold down Shift and then choose the File menu's Close All command.

continues

Closing Documents *(continued)*

Word watches for unsaved changes

Word won't close a document you've changed but not yet saved. It first asks whether you want to save your changes. If you indicate that you do want to save your changes, Word effectively chooses the File menu's Save command for you.

SEE ALSO Saving Documents

Collect And Copy

Collect And Copy refers to a new feature in Microsoft Office 2000 that lets you store more than one copied or cut selection on the Windows **Clipboard**. Word, predictably, supports the Collect And Copy feature.

Coloring Documents

You can color the selected document's background area. This changes the document color on the screen and, if you print the document with a color-capable printer, changes the printed colors too.

Adding Background Color to a Document

To add background colors to the selected document area, follow these steps:

1. Choose the Format menu's Borders And Shading command.
2. Click the Shading tab.
3. Select a shading percentage from the Style list box.
4. Choose the shading color in the Color drop-down list box.
5. Click in the Fill palette the background color you want.

Removing Color from a Document

To return the selected document area's color to the default color scheme—the always-popular black on white—follow these steps:

1. Choose the Format menu's Borders And Shading command.
2. Click the Shading tab.
3. Click the down arrow to open the Color drop-down list box.
4. Click the Automatic selection.
5. Click the down arrow to open the Patterns drop-down list box.
6. Click the Clear selection.
7. Click No Fill in the Fill Palette.

If your audience includes men

As many as 1 in 12 males has what's commonly described as "color blindness." If your audience includes males, therefore, consider avoiding the red-green color combinations that many males have trouble differentiating.

SEE ALSO Coloring Text; Formatting

Coloring Text

You can color the **characters** in the current **document** selection. As you might guess, any change of character color shows up on your screen if you have a color monitor. The change shows up in your printed documents too, if you have a color-capable printer.

Adding Color to Characters

To change the color of the characters in the current document selection, follow these steps:

1. Choose the Format menu's Font command.
2. Click the Font tab.
3. Click the down arrow to open the Font Color drop-down list box.
4. Click the color you want.

continues

Coloring Text *(continued)*

Removing Color from Characters

To change the color of the characters in the current document selection to basic black (the usual default color), follow these steps:

1. Choose the Format menu's Font command.
2. Click the Font tab.
3. Click the down arrow to open the Font Color drop-down list box.
4. Click Automatic.

Color contrast affects legibility

As you start working with color, you should know that publishers, such as Microsoft Press, have a reason for using black ink on white paper: Black on white provides for maximum contrast and, therefore, maximum legibility. Whenever you decrease the contrast, you reduce legibility.

SEE ALSO Highlighting Text

Column Breaks

You can choose where Word breaks, or ends, one **column** of text and starts a new column. (Word starts the new column either adjacent to the old column or on a new page.)

To do this, place the **insertion point** where you want the break. Then choose the Insert menu's Break command, and click Column Break. In Normal view, Word draws a dotted line and writes the words *Column Break* on the line to show where column breaks occur.

Columns

Some documents use more than one column of text on a page. Newspapers do this, for example, and so do many newsletters and magazines.

You can specify that Word print several columns of text on a page by choosing the Format menu's Columns command. When Word displays the Columns dialog box, indicate how many columns you want by using the Number Of Columns list box or the Presets options. You can also control the size and arrangement of the columns by using the Width and Spacing options.

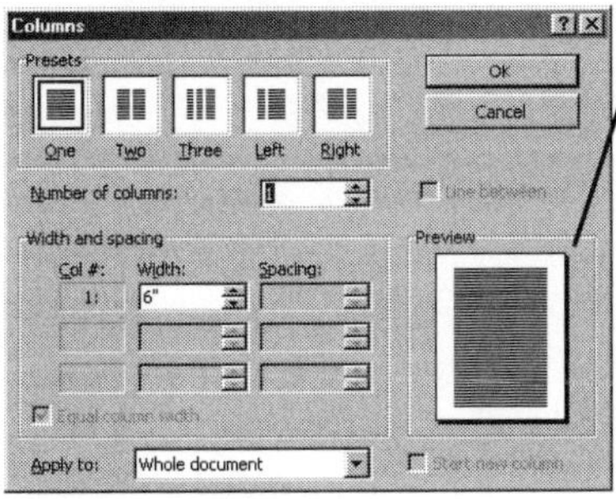

As you work with the Columns dialog box, you can use the Preview area to see what your changes do to your document. When you click OK to make your changes, you can see the columns as they will print by choosing the View menu's Page Layout command.

SEE ALSO Column Breaks

Combining Files

You can insert a file—including a Word document—into the active document, which means that you can easily combine documents. To insert a file in a document, follow these steps:

1 Position the **insertion point** at the document location where the file should be inserted.

2 Choose the Insert menu's File command. Word displays the Insert File dialog box.

continues

Combining Files *(continued)*

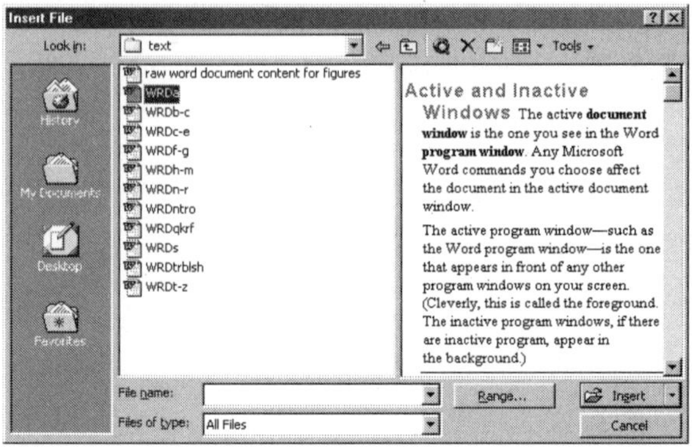

3 Select a file type from the Files Of Type drop-down list box.

4 Click the **History, My Documents, Desktop,** or **Favorites** shortcut icon to specify where the document is located if you've previously saved, opened, or viewed the file; stored it in the My Documents folder; stored it on your desktop; or added it to your Favorites folder. Alternatively, use the Look In boxes to specify where the file is located.

5 Select your file or type its name in the File Name box, and then click Insert.

SEE ALSO Opening Documents; Saving Documents

Comments

Comments are annotations, or notes, you've added to a document. Although the comments are part of the document file—people can view the comments as they review the document on-screen, for example—the document can be viewed and printed without comments.

Adding Comments

To add a comment, first position the insertion point after the sentence or the **paragraph** where you want to add a note. Then choose the Insert menu's Comment command. Word opens a Comment pane at the bottom of the **document window**, which you use to type your comments.

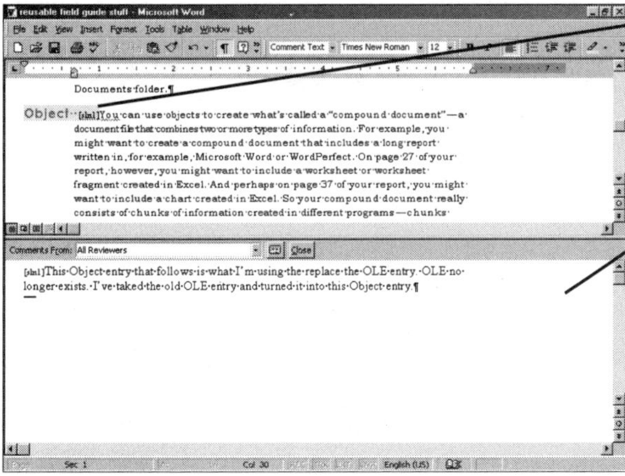

To flag the comment, Word labels it with the user's initials and a sequential number.

Type your comments in the Comment pane.

Deleting Comments

To delete a comment, select its marker and press Delete. To show the comment markers, choose the View menu's Comments command or click the Show/Hide ¶ toolbar button.

Control Menu Commands

Control menu commands appear on the Control menus of **program windows, document windows,** and **dialog boxes.** To open the Control menu of a window or a dialog box, click the Control menu box. (It's the little logo in the upper left corner of the window or the dialog box.) Control menu commands let you manipulate the window or the dialog box in a variety of ways, as described in the table on the next page:

continues

Control Menu Commands *(continued)*

Command	What it does
Restore	Undoes the last minimize or maximize action.
Move	Tells Windows that you want to move the window or the dialog box. When you choose this command, Windows changes the mouse pointer to a four-headed arrow. When this happens, use the direction keys to change the screen position of the window or the dialog box.
Size	Tells Windows that you want to change the size of the window. When you choose this command, Windows changes the mouse pointer to a four-headed arrow. You change the window size by using the Up and Down direction keys to move the top border and by using the Left and Right direction keys to move the left border.
Minimize	Tells Windows that it should remove the window from the screen. Windows follows your command but, to remind you of the minimized window, displays a small bar. If you minimize a document window, the small bar appears at the bottom of the program window. If you minimize an application window, the small bar appears on the Taskbar. To see the Control menu of a minimized window, simply click its visible control icon.
Maximize	Tells Windows that it should make the window or the dialog box as big as it can. If you maximize the Word program window, Windows makes the program window as big as your screen. In Word, by the way, document windows are maximized so that they fill the program window.
Close	Removes the window or the dialog box from the screen. There's more to this command than first meets the eye, however. If you close a program window, you close the program and any files that might be open in that program. If you close a document window, you close only the document displayed in the document window. If the document hasn't yet been saved, Word will ask whether you want to save it before closing the document. If you close a dialog box, it's the same as selecting Cancel.

Control menu commands' availability

You won't always see all these commands on a Control menu. Windows displays only the commands that make sense in the current situation.

SEE ALSO **Closing Documents**

Copying Formatting

You can copy the formatting you've assigned to a character or to a **paragraph** by using Format Painter. To copy formatting, select the character or paragraph with the formatting you want to copy, click the Format Painter toolbar button, and then drag the mouse over the characters or paragraphs you want formatted.

The amount of formatting the Format Painter tool copies depends on what you select before clicking the toolbar button. If you select a character or a set of characters, Format Painter copies only character formatting—such as font styles and **point sizes.** If you select a paragraph, Format Painter copies both character formatting and paragraph formatting.

Copying Tables

You can copy the tables you create in Word. To do this, click a table cell and then choose the Table menu's Select Table command. Next, choose the Edit menu's Copy command. When you later want to paste the table, position the insertion point at the exact point where you want the table and then choose the Edit menu's Paste command.

SEE ALSO **Creating Tables; Drag-and-Drop**

Copying Text

Word lets you copy the text you have in a document. All you need to do is select the text—for example, by clicking or dragging—and then choose the Edit menu's Copy command. To move the copied text to a new location, reposition the **insertion point** where you want the text to be copied and then choose the Edit menu's Paste command. Word copies the text and any formatting you've assigned to it.

SEE ALSO Copying Formatting; Copying Tables; Copying Text Without Formatting; Drag-and-Drop; Selecting

Copying Text Without Formatting

When you copy text in the usual way, by using the Edit menu's Copy and Paste commands, Word copies both the text and any formatting you've assigned to the text. You can, however, copy text without formatting. To copy text without formatting, follow these steps:

1 Select the text.
2 Choose the Edit menu's Copy command.
3 Position the insertion point where you want to copy the unformatted text.
4 Choose the Edit menu's Paste Special command. Word displays the Paste Special dialog box.

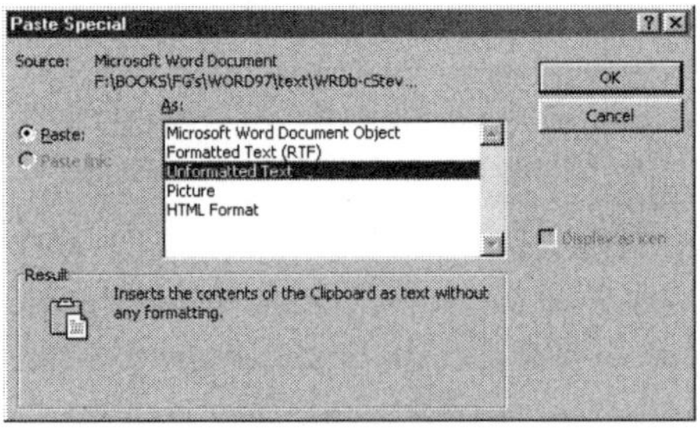

5 Select Unformatted Text from the list box, and then click OK.

SEE ALSO Moving Pictures; Resizing Pictures

Creating Styles

You can create **styles** in several ways, but the easiest way is to format a paragraph so that it includes all the **font, paragraph,** tab, **border, frame,** language, and numbering formats you want to combine in a style. Then select the paragraph, click the down arrow to open the Style box on the Personal **toolbar,** type the name you want to give the style, and press Enter.

SEE ALSO Applying Styles; Changing Styles; Formatting

Creating Tables

Word lets you easily add a **table** to a **document**—and, in fact, provides two methods for doing so. You can either draw a table (the method most people find easiest) or insert a table.

Drawing a Table

To draw a table, follow these steps:

1 Choose the Table menu's Draw Table command. When you do this, Word charges the cursor to a pencil.

2 Point to the place where you want the table's top left corner to rest, and then drag the cursor to the place where you want the table's bottom right corner to rest. When you release the mouse, Word draws the outside edge of the table.

3 To break the table's interior into rows, draw the rows. To draw a row, point to the left edge of the table and then drag the cursor to the right edge of the table.

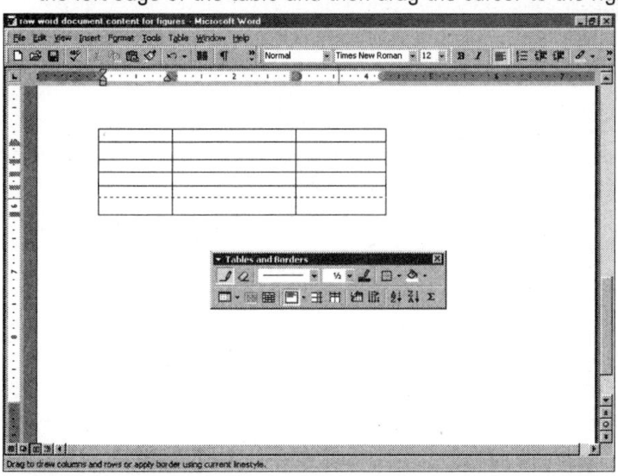

4 To break the table's interior into columns, draw the columns. To draw a column, point to the top edge of the table and then drag the cursor to the bottom edge of the table.

continues

Creating Tables *(continued)*

Inserting a Table

To insert a table, follow these steps:

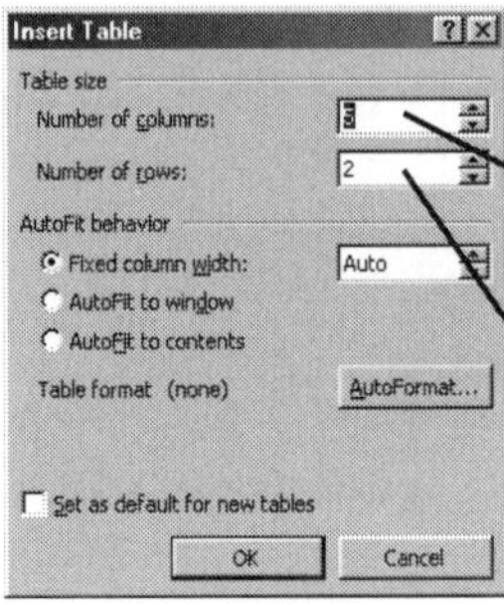

1. Choose the Table menu's Insert command, and then choose the submenu's Table command.
2. Tell Word how many columns you want. Don't worry about being too precise. It's easy to add columns (and rows) later on.
3. Tell Word how many rows you want, and then click OK. Word inserts the table.

Filling a Table

To fill in the table, simply click the cells and type whatever you want. Note that you can use Word tables like miniature spreadsheets. For example, you can enter formulas in cells that reference the values in other cells.

Working with the Tables And Borders Toolbar

If you use the Draw Table command to create a table, Word displays the Tables And Borders toolbar. You can also tell Word to display this toolbar by choosing the View menu's Toolbars command and then choosing the submenu's Tables And Borders command. This toolbar provides many useful toolbar buttons for working with a newly created table. Draw Table lets you indicate that you want to draw additional rows and columns, for example. Eraser lets you remove rows and column edges, thereby removing rows and columns. Line Style, Line Weight, and Border Column let you specify what the borders that make up the table should look like. Outside Border lets you draw a table border around the outside edge of the table. Note that you can learn the name of any Tables And Borders toolbar button by pointing to it. With the name in hand, you can usually determine (or guess) what a particular toolbar button does. If you still have questions, ask the **Office Assistant**.

Cursor

The cursor is the icon that moves across the Word program window as you type or move the mouse. Word changes what the cursor looks like depending on what you're doing. In this book, I usually refer to the cursor as an **insertion point.**

Datasheet

A datasheet is the worksheet you use when you create a Microsoft Graph object. Typically, you enter data in a datasheet when you create a new graph object by using the Insert menu's Object command. You can also move the data in a table to a datasheet. To do this, simply select the table before you choose the Insert menu's Object command.

Dates

You can enter a field for the current system date by pressing Alt+Shift+D. Word enters the date at the insertion point in MM/DD/YY format. If it's October 7, 1999, for example, Word enters 10/7/99.

If you want to pick a different format, you can also use the Insert menu's Date And Time command, but you need to select the Update Automatically check box to make the date a field. As a field, the date is updated automatically. Note that you can manually update a date field you've inserted in a document by clicking the field and then pressing F9.

SEE ALSO **Field Codes; Times**

Deleting

Deleting comments SEE **Comments**

Deleting files SEE **Erasing Documents**

Deleting text SEE **Erasing**

Removing table columns and rows SEE **Deleting Columns and Rows**

Removing footnotes and endnotes SEE **Footnotes and Endnotes**

Removing revision marks SEE **Revisions**

Deleting Columns and Rows

To delete columns or rows from a **table**, click a cell in the column or row you want to delete. Select the column or row by choosing the Table menu's Select Column or Select Row command. Then choose the Table menu's Delete Rows or Delete Columns command.

SEE ALSO **Creating Tables**

Desktop

The desktop is what you see when you start Windows. It's the desktop, for example, that provides shortcut icons and on which the Start button and Taskbar rest. This desktop doesn't directly have anything to do with Word—except that both the Open Document and Save Document dialog boxes let you easily store and retrieve Word documents there.

Detect And Repair

Microsoft Office programs such as Word provide a Detect And Repair command on their Help menus. You can choose this command to direct an Office program, such as Word, to look for and, if possible, repair programs with noncritical files. (An example of a noncritical file is a missing or corrupt font file.) Note that Word automatically identifies and repairs problems with critical files.

Document Map

If you use the Word heading styles in your document, the Document Map displays a pane to the left of the document window with an outline of the document's structure. Use it to take in at a glance the gist of a long or online document or to keep track of your place in the document.

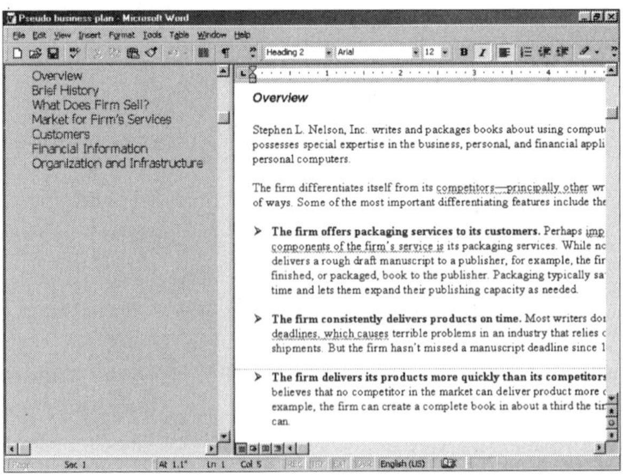

To use the Word Document Map, first make sure that you've applied the Word heading styles to the headings and subheadings in your document. Then choose the View menu's Document Map command, or click the Document Map toolbar button. After you do this, you can browse the document in the usual way. As you move the insertion point through the document, the Document Map selects the heading for your current location in the document. To turn off the Document Map, choose the View menu's Document Map command again.

Using custom heading styles

Word's Document Map, Outline, and Master Document features work best if you use Word's Heading 1, Heading 2, and Heading 3 styles for your headings and subheadings. If these styles don't suit your needs, you can solve this dilemma by using these styles and modifying their appearance and other characteristics. To do this, choose the Format menu's Style command, select the name of the style you want to change, and then click Modify. Change whatever you want about the style (except its name). Now you have the best of both worlds. For more about customizing styles, see **Changing Styles**.

SEE ALSO Applying Styles

Documents

A document is what you see in the white area of the Word window. A document includes the text you type, the pictures you add, and the **tables** you build. You store documents as separate files on your disk.

SEE ALSO Opening Documents; Saving Documents

Document Template SEE Templates

Document Views

You can look at a document on the screen in several ways by choosing the View menu's Normal, Web Layout, Print Layout, and Outline commands. You can also use the View buttons to flip-flop between Normal, Web Layout, Print Layout, and Outline views. The View buttons appear at the left end of the horizontal scroll bar, near the bottom left corner of the Word program window. The following table describes these views:

View	Description
Normal view	Displays a document as a long, uninterrupted column of text, pictures, tables, and whatever else you've added.
Web Layout view	Shows how your document will look online.
Print Layout view	Shows how your document would look printed on pages; you can also add headers and footers by using this view.
Outline view	Shows a document as an outline built from your headings.

SEE ALSO Document Map; Outlining

Document Window

The document window is the rectangular area in which Word displays your **documents.** If you have more than one document open, each document is displayed in its own window. To arrange the windows so they don't overlap, choose the Window menu's Arrange All command.

SEE ALSO Control Menu Commands

Drag-and-Drop

Drag-and-drop is a technique that lets you move and copy pieces of a document with the mouse. To move some piece of a document—such as a line of text, a paragraph, or a picture—select it, drag it to its new location, and release the mouse button. To copy some piece of a document—such as a block of text or a picture—select it, press Ctrl, drag it to its new location, and release the mouse button.

Drawing

Word comes with a Drawing **toolbar,** which you can use to draw simple hand-drawn images in your **documents.** Even if you're not an artist or graphics designer, using the Word Drawing tools is simple and straightforward enough that you may be able to draw objects of surprising quality.

Adding Drawn Objects to a Document

To add a hand-drawn graphics image to a document, click the Drawing toolbar button, or choose the View menu's Toolbars command and then choose the submenu's Drawing command. Word displays its Drawing toolbar at the bottom of the program window. Click its buttons to draw many different kinds of shapes and to position them, color them, and give them three-dimensional effects.

Using the Draw Menu

Click the Draw toolbar button to display a menu of commands to position drawn objects, place them in relation to a nonprinting grid, group or ungroup objects, rotate or flip objects, or modify the shapes of drawn objects. The following table describes the Draw menu commands:

Command	Description
Group	Combines the set of selected drawn objects into a single object. To select the drawing objects you want to group, hold down Shift and then click each object.
Ungroup	Separates previously grouped drawn objects. To use this command, click an object in the group and then choose the command.
Regroup	Joins ungrouped drawn objects back to their previous group.
Order	Displays a submenu of commands you can use to move the selected drawing object in front of or behind other overlapping objects or to bring drawing objects in front of text or behind text.
Grid	Displays a dialog box you use to specify whether to snap drawn objects to a nonprinting grid, set the placement and spacing of the grid, and snap objects to other objects.
Nudge	Moves the selected drawn objects by small increments.

continues

Drawing *(continued)*

Command	Description
Align Or Distribute	Lines up drawn objects in relation to each other or in relation to the page. To select multiple drawing objects so that they can be aligned, hold down Shift while clicking the objects. Note that when Word aligns a single drawn object, it aligns the object against the page edge, although this command gives you the choice of aligning the objects relative to one another.
Rotate Or Flip	Displays a submenu of commands you use to rotate the drawn object freely, rotate it left or right 45 degrees, or flip-flop the drawing object horizontally or vertically.
Text Wrapping	Displays a submenu of commands you use to specify the way text wraps an object.
Edit Points	Lets you change the shape of drawn objects made up of multiple lines or arrows. After you choose the command, drag the connecting points to move them.
Change AutoShape	Displays a box of AutoShapes you can choose from to replace the selected drawn object's AutoShape.
Set AutoShape Defaults	Specifies the default color and other effects used for any new AutoShapes you create.

Selecting Objects

You can typically select drawing objects you want to manipulate by simply clicking them. If you've already clicked another toolbar button and Word expects you to do something other than select a drawing object, click the Drawing toolbar's Select Objects button to indicate that you want to select a drawing object.

Free-Rotating Drawn Objects

You can manually rotate the selected drawn object by using the Drawing toolbar's Free Rotate tool. After you click the toolbar button, the mouse pointer changes to include a rotation symbol, and the object's handles become round. To rotate the object, grab a handle with the mouse and drag either clockwise or counterclockwise.

Using AutoShapes

You can add AutoShape drawn objects to a document by clicking AutoShape, selecting an AutoShape category from the AutoShape menu, and then selecting an AutoShape from the box that Word displays.

Drawing Lines, Arrows, Rectangles, and Ellipses

The Drawing toolbar provides Line, Arrow, Rectangle, Oval, and Text Box toolbar buttons for adding these other drawing objects to your documents. Most of these tools work in predictable ways.

The Line and Arrow tools work similarly to each other. To use the Line tool, for example, click the Line toolbar button, and then click where you want the line to start, dragging the mouse where you want the line to end. To use the Arrow tool, click the Arrow toolbar button, and then click where you want the tail of the arrow, dragging the mouse to where you want the pointed end of the arrow.

To use the Rectangle tool, click the Rectangle toolbar button. Next, click where you want the upper left corner of the rectangle. Then drag the mouse to where you want the lower right corner of the rectangle. To draw a square, hold down the Shift key as you drag the mouse.

To use the Oval tool, click the Oval toolbar button. Next, pretend to draw an invisible rectangle that just fits the oval by clicking one corner of the rectangle and dragging the mouse to the opposite corner of the rectangle. If you want a circle, hold down the Shift key while dragging the mouse.

Creating Text Boxes

To create a text box, click the Text Box toolbar button, click where you want the upper left corner of the text box, and then drag the mouse to where you want the lower right corner of the text box. Next, type the text in your text box. The text wraps to fit the box; if you decide that you want to change the size or shape of the text box, drag its handles.

Adding WordArt to a Drawing

Click the Insert **WordArt** toolbar button to start WordArt.

Coloring Drawn Objects

The Drawing toolbar provides three tools for coloring drawn objects: Fill Color, Line Color, and Font Color. Click the Fill Color toolbar button to change the interior colors of drawn objects. Click the Line Color toolbar button to change the color of borders and lines for drawn objects. Click the Font Color toolbar button to change the color of text in drawn objects.

continues

Drawing *(continued)*

Changing Line and Arrow Appearance

The Drawing toolbar also provides three tools for controlling the way lines and arrows look: Line Style, Dash Style, and Arrow Style. Click the Line Style toolbar button to change the thickness of the lines you draw or to make lines double or triple width. Click the Dash Style toolbar button to select a solid or broken line style. Click the Arrow Style toolbar button to choose a style for your arrowheads. (If you want a fancier arrow, click the AutoShapes toolbar button, choose Block Arrows, and select an arrow from the gallery.)

Using Shadows and Three-Dimensional Effects

The Drawing toolbar provides two tools for adding shadows and three-dimensional effects to drawn objects: Click the Shadow toolbar button to give a drawn object a shadow. (Whatever shadow style you choose, don't get too dramatic about mixing shadow types in a drawing. Being consistent with shadows, as though all objects in the drawing are being lit by the same light source, usually looks best.) Click the 3-D toolbar button to give a drawn object a faux 3-D effect. (Again, be careful about how you mix perspectives or else the results will look strange.)

Drop Caps

A dropped capital letter, or drop cap, is sometimes used as the first letter in a document. You often see a dropped capital letter at the beginning of mystery novels, for example. You can make the selected character a drop cap by choosing the Format menu's Drop Cap command.

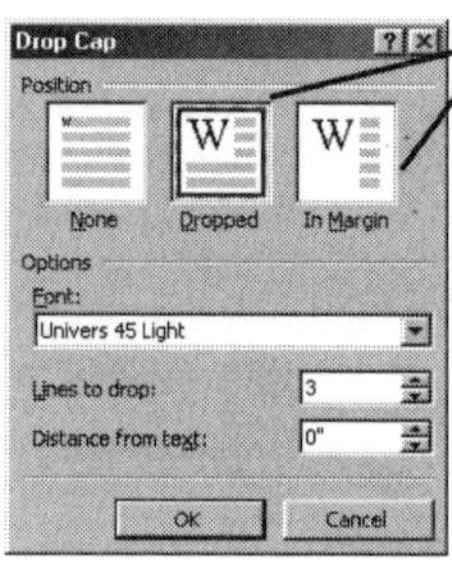

Select either the Dropped or In Margin option. Note that the Drop Cap dialog box lets you specify some other font, select a drop depth in lines, and specify how far from the text the drop letter should be placed.

SEE ALSO Changing Fonts; Fonts

Editing Tables

The cells in tables are easy to edit.

Replacing Cell Contents

Click the cell near its left edge. Word selects the entire cell's contents. You can replace the contents by typing.

Editing Cell Contents

In the cell, click where you want to place the **insertion point.** Then edit the cell's contents in the usual way: typing, deleting, and backspacing, for example.

Editing Text

To edit text you've already entered, first select the character or the block of text you want to change. (Click just before the first character you want to change, and then drag the mouse to just after the last character you want to change.) Next, type the new text that you want to replace the old text.

Overtyping

Normally, Word inserts the characters you type at the **insertion point** location. You can tell Word to replace, or overtype, characters that follow the insertion point by pressing Insert or by double-clicking OVR on the status bar. Word then displays the OVR indicator on the status bar in bold. Any text you type will replace existing text, starting with the character just to the right of the insertion point. To turn off overtyping, press Insert or double-click OVR again.

SEE ALSO Entering Text

E-Mail

You may be able to e-mail the active Word document to someone else by choosing the File menu's Send To command and then the submenu's Mail Recipient (As Attachment) command. When you choose this command, Windows starts your e-mail program and attaches the active document to the message. To complete the message, just supply the recipient's e-mail name and click the Send toolbar button. Note that Word doesn't provide this command unless it knows that you have e-mail service.

Embedding and Linking Existing Objects

To create an object from an existing file, follow these steps:

1. Choose the Insert menu's Object command.
2. Click the Create From File tab.

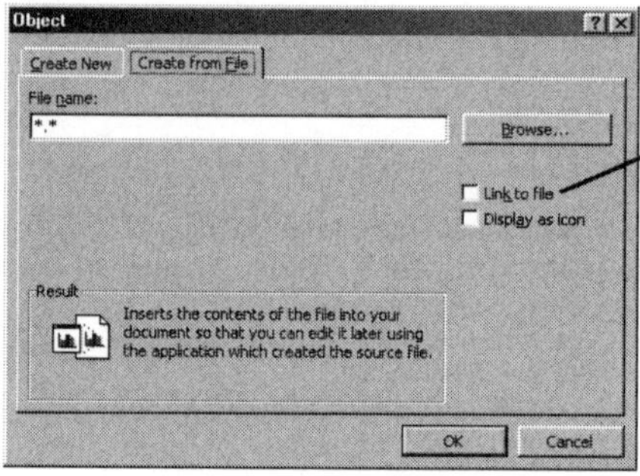

If you don't check the Link To File box, Word embeds a copy of the file.

3. If you know the name of the file where the object is located, type it in the File Name box and then skip to step 7. Otherwise, click Browse.
4. Select a file type from the Files Of Type drop-down list box.
5. Open the Look In drop-down list box, and search the list of folders beneath it to identify the folder where the file is located.
6. Select the file, and then click Insert.
7. On the Create From File tab, select the Link To File check box if you want Windows to automatically update the object whenever changes are made in the file.
8. Select the Display As Icon check box if you want Word to display the object as an icon rather than as a picture.
9. Click OK.

Embedding New Objects

To create an **object** from scratch in an application other than Word, follow the steps on the next page:

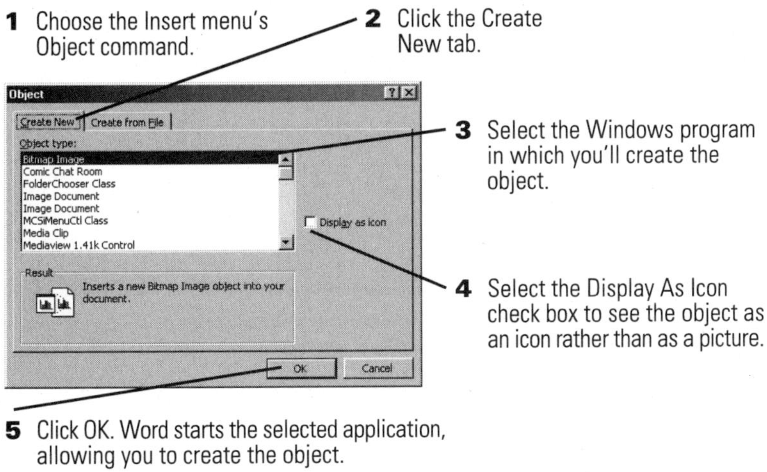

End-of-Document Markers

Under the last line of **documents** in some **document views,** Word places a thick, quarter-inch-long underline character. This character, called the end-of-document marker, identifies your document's last line.

Usually you don't need to concern yourself with the end-of-document marker. However, in one situation, knowing about the end-of-document marker can be quite useful. If extra blank pages are printing at the end of each and every document, it may be that you've accumulated paragraph breaks at the end of the document and are printing the paragraph breaks. In this case, the end-of-document marker won't be under your last line of text; it'll be separated from that line by a bunch of empty lines.

Ending Lines

You normally don't have to worry about ending lines of text. Word automatically wraps your lines. If you want to end a line of text without ending a **paragraph**, however, you can do so by pressing Shift+Enter.

Carriage returns

Don't press Enter (the Return key) at the end of a line; Word moves the **insertion point** to the next line when it runs out of room. Word also moves words from one line to the next line if there isn't room. This feature is called **word wrap**.

Endnotes

In Word, you add, modify, and delete endnotes the same way as you do footnotes.

SEE ALSO **Footnote and Endnote Options; Footnotes and Endnotes**

Entering Text

To enter text in a **document**, you typically use the keyboard to type the **characters**. However, you can also easily **copy text** from another document by using the **Clipboard** or by choosing the Insert menu's File command, as described in the **Combining Files** entry.

Envelopes

You can print an envelope with Word as long as your printer accepts envelopes. To do so, follow the steps on the next page:

1 If you're typing a document that already includes the person's name and address, select them.

2 Choose the Tools menu's Envelopes And Labels command.

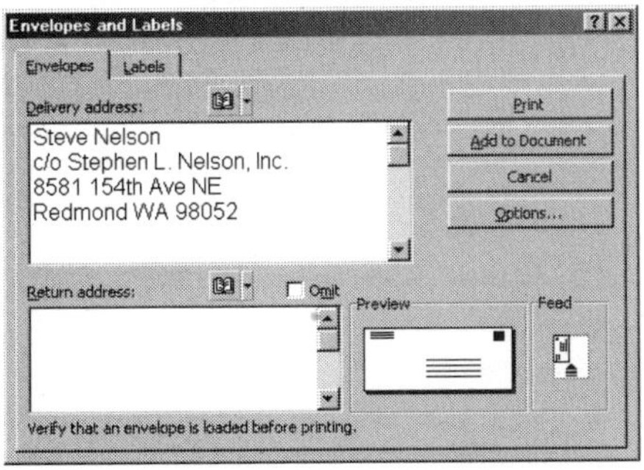

3 If necessary, type the name and address of the person to whom you want the post office to deliver your letter. (Word fills this box with whatever you selected in step 1, so you may not need to change its contents if you completed that step.)

4 If you're not using preprinted envelopes that already show your return address, enter this information in the Return Address box. If you don't want to print the return address, select the Omit check box.

5 Confirm that the Preview box shows how you want your envelope to look. (If the Preview box is wrong, repeat steps 3 and 4.)

6 If you haven't already done so, insert the envelope into your printer the way it expects it, as shown by the Feed box.

7 When you're ready, click Print. Word prints your envelope.

Erasing

You can erase the current selection—a **character,** a **paragraph,** a picture, a **table,** or some combination of these document parts—by pressing Delete or by choosing the Edit menu's Clear command. You can erase the preceding character or the current selection by pressing Backspace.

Erasing fields

You can't Backspace over fields—even when a field includes a single character. To erase a field, select the entire field and then press Delete or choose the Edit menu's Clear command. A field, by the way, is simply an instruction to Word to insert something into your document.

SEE ALSO Field Codes

Erasing Documents

Documents are files that are stored on disk. To erase a file, therefore, you use either Windows Explorer or My Computer. Whichever method you choose, highlight the filename you want to erase and then right-click it. Choose the shortcut menu's Delete command. When Windows asks whether you really want to delete the document, click Yes.

If you accidentally erase a document

You should know that it's possible to recover a document you've deleted. In fact, it's quite easy. Double-click the Recycle Bin icon on the Windows desktop. In the Recycle Bin window, highlight the document you want to recover, and then choose the File menu's Restore command. The file is put right back in the folder you erased it from. The Recycle Bin can hold only so many files, however. If you erased a long time ago the file you want to recover, it might not be in the Recycle Bin anymore.

Excel

You can use Microsoft Excel worksheets and charts in your Word documents. In Excel, select the worksheet range or chart, and then choose the Edit menu's Copy command. Switch to the Word application, position the insertion point at the location where you want the worksheet or chart, and choose the Edit menu's Paste command.

SEE ALSO **Object; Switching Tasks**

Exiting Word

To exit from Word—or from just about any other Windows program—choose the File menu's Exit command. Or you can close the Word program window—for example, by clicking its Close button. Word will ask whether you want to save documents that have unsaved changes.

SEE ALSO **Closing Documents; Saving Documents; Window Buttons**

Exporting Documents

Exporting means copying a document so that you or someone else can use it with another program—usually another word processing program, such as WordPerfect. You export a Word document by saving the file in a format the other program can use. To save a file in another format, choose the File menu's Save As command and select the format from the Save As Type drop-down list box.

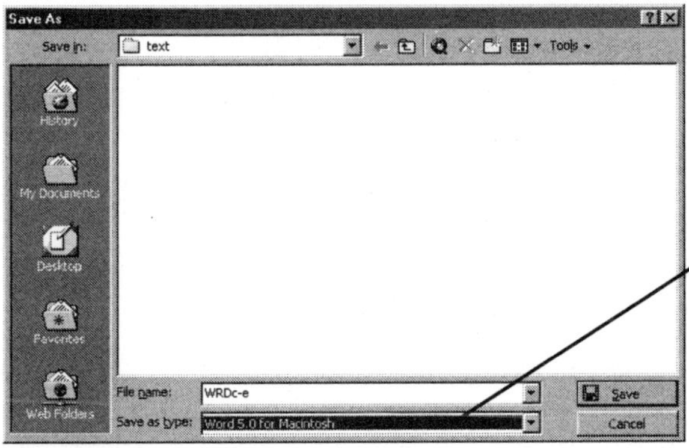

To export a document file, save the file in a format the other program can open.

SEE ALSO Saving Documents; WordPerfect

Choosing an export file format

If you can't find a file format that matches the application to which you want to export the document, use either rich-text format or one of the straight-text file formats. Note that if you use a straight-text file format, you may not be able to export the document formatting, but you'll be able to export the document text.

Favorites

Windows will maintain a list of your favorite web pages. Although you create this list of favorites with Windows or Microsoft Internet Explorer, the favorites list is relevant to Word. Both the Open Documents dialog box and the Save Documents dialog box provide a Favorites shortcut icon, which you can click to display the favorites list.

Field Codes

Field codes are really instructions you've entered (or that Word has entered) in a **document.** You enter field codes, for example, to direct Word to add a term to the **index** or to add a heading to the **table of contents.** You enter field codes to direct Word to calculate **formulas.**

Entering Field Codes

Enter field codes in documents by choosing the Insert menu's Field command.

Viewing Field Codes

To see the field codes in a document—Word usually shows the field results—click the Show/Hide ¶ toolbar button.

Figure Captions

Do you ever put figures in your documents? If you do and you want to tag the figures with captions, use the Insert Caption command, which, in essence, lets you connect captions to the figures they describe.

Adding Figure Captions

To add a caption to a figure, select the figure, choose the Insert menu's Caption command, and then follow these steps:

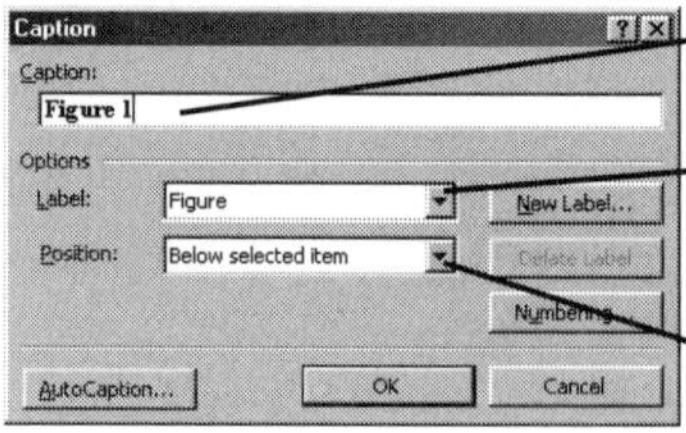

1. Enter the caption in the Caption text box.
2. Identify what you're labeling in the Label drop-down list box as either a figure, a table, or an equation.
3. Select a position for the caption from the Position drop-down list box.

SEE ALSO Text Boxes

Filenames

You give a **document** its filename when you choose the File menu's Save As command.

Filename Rules

A filename can be as long as 256 characters. A filename may use any number or letter and many other symbol characters. You can't, however, use symbol characters that Windows expects to be used in special ways on its command line, such as asterisks and question marks. Note that if you violate a file-naming rule, Windows just alerts you to the error and allows you to make the necessary correction.

Specifying File Extensions

The file extension, by the way, isn't something you need to worry about. Windows and Word use file extensions to identify the file type. You can accept the default Word document file type, DOC. Or you can choose the File menu's Save As command, and then select another file type from the Save As Type drop-down list box.

SEE ALSO Save Options; Saving Documents

File Properties

In addition to the **text,** pictures, and **tables** stored in a **document,** you can store additional information that describes the document itself and makes it easier to find. To collect and store additional information, follow these steps:

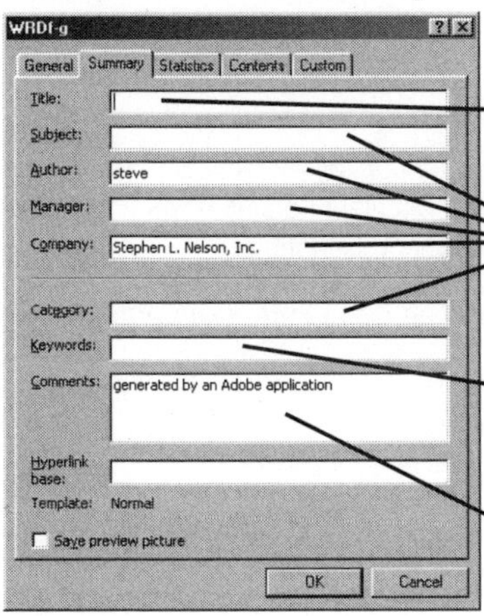

1. Choose the File menu's Properties command.
2. Give a lengthy, full, descriptive title to your document by using the Title text box.
3. Identify the document subject matter and author and, if you want, a manager name, company name, and category.
4. Optionally, add keywords that will make it easy to find the document file later by choosing the Tools menu's Find command.
5. Optionally, type additional information about the document file in the Comments box.

Finding Files

Word supplies a powerful Find File tool for locating documents you've misplaced. You use this command to search for documents having specified **file properties.** To use the Find command, follow these steps:

1. Choose the File menu's Open command.
2. Click Tools. When Word opens the Tools menu, choose the Find command. Word displays the Find dialog box.

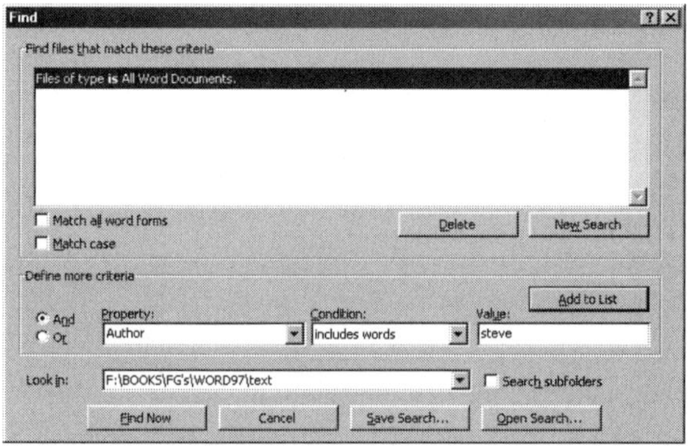

3. Initially, Find assumes that it will look for any Word document. But you can use the Define More Criteria options—Property, Condition, and Value—to outline additional search rules Find should use. The Property box lets you specify what characteristic of the document—such as the author name—you want the Find command to look at. The Condition and Value boxes let you specify what the Property value should look like. When you finish specifying a search rule, click Add To List. Note that you can add more than one rule.
4. Select an option from the Look In drop-down list box and select the Search Subfolders check box to specify where Word should look for the misplaced documents.
5. Click Find Now to direct Word to look for documents that match your description. Word redisplays the Open Document dialog box, this time listing any documents it finds that match your description.

SEE ALSO Troubleshooting: You Can't Find a Document

Finding Formatting

You can search for formatting. To do so, follow these steps:

1 Choose the Edit menu's Find command.

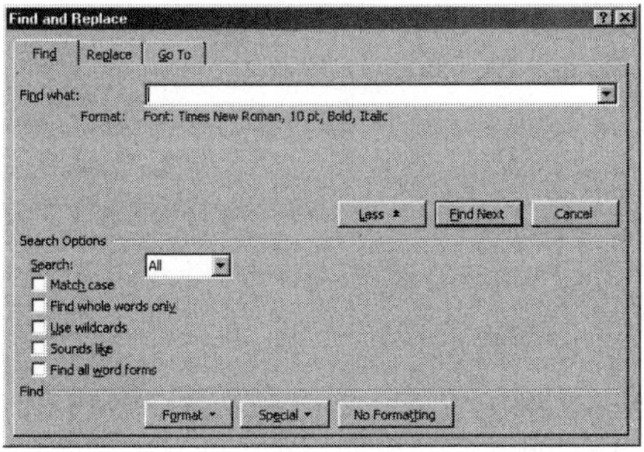

2 If necessary, click More to display more options, and then click Format. Word lists the types of formatting.

3 Select a formatting type from the list. Word displays another dialog box.

4 Describe the type of formatting you're looking for.

SEE ALSO Finding Text

Finding Text

You can use the Edit menu's Find command to locate words, phrases, and other fragments of **text** in a **document.** To use the Find command, follow these steps:

1 To search a specific part of the document, select that area beforehand, or don't select anything if you want Word to search the entire document.

2 Choose the Edit menu's Find command. If necessary, click More to see all the options.

continues

Finding Text *(continued)*

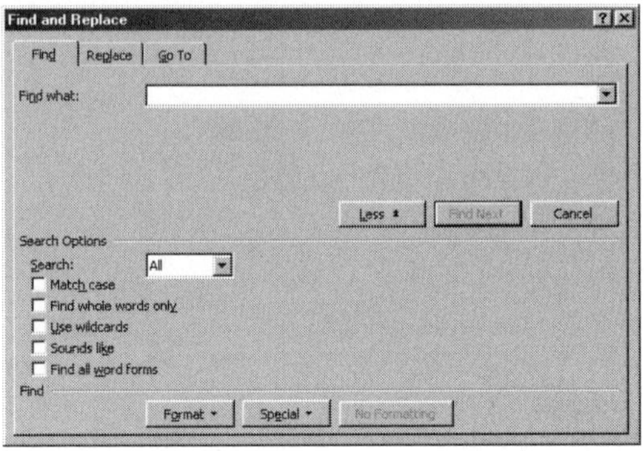

3 Enter text in the Find What box to specify what it is you're looking for.

4 Select a direction in the Search drop-down list box to indicate in which direction Word should search.

5 Select the Match Case and Find Whole Words Only check boxes to indicate whether Word should consider case (lowercase vs. uppercase) in its search and look for only whole words rather than parts of words.

6 Select the Sounds Like check box to find words that are pronounced like the Find What text: "their" and "there," "you're" and "your," and "are" and "our," for example.

7 Select the Find All Word Forms check box to find words based on the same root word you entered in the Find What box.

SEE ALSO Finding Formatting; Replacing Text

Font Animation

You can add movement, or animation, to document text—an effect that can work well when you're creating a document for online or screen display. To animate a text selection, choose the Format menu's Font command and then click the Text Effects tab. Select your choice in the Animations box, and then watch the Preview box for a demonstration of Vegas lights, marching red or black ants, letters that shimmer or sparkle, or whatever. When you've found an effect you like, click OK to apply it.

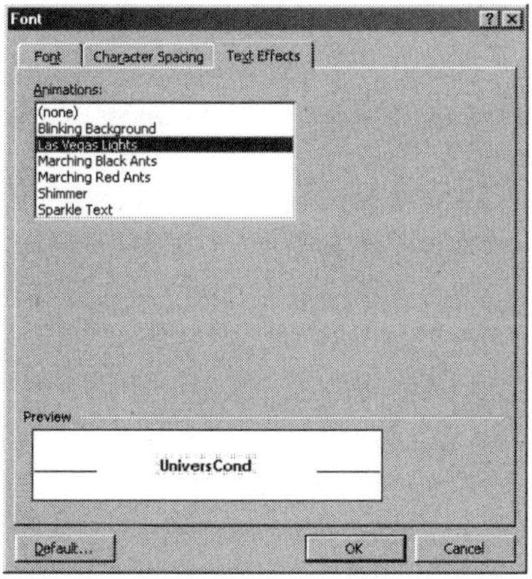

SEE ALSO Changing Fonts; Fonts

Fonts

Word lets you use a wide variety of fonts in your documents. With fonts, you can even add Greek symbols and other special characters to your document. Here are a few examples:

Arial resembles Helvetica.

Courier New looks like typewriter output.

Times New Roman uses serifs—little cross strokes—to make characters easier to read.

☎ ✝ ✈ ❽ ❦ — These are TrueType Wingding characters

✝✝✝✝✝✝✝✝✝

SEE ALSO Changing Fonts; Font Animation

Footers

Page footers can be added to the bottom of printed documents. You typically use footers to include information such as publication dates, page numbers, and confidentiality notices.

SEE ALSO Headers and Footers

Footnote and Endnote Options

Word gives you significant control over where and how it locates **footnotes and endnotes** and how it numbers these notes. To exercise this control, choose the Insert menu's Footnote command. When Word displays the Footnote And Endnote dialog box, click Options and then follow these steps:

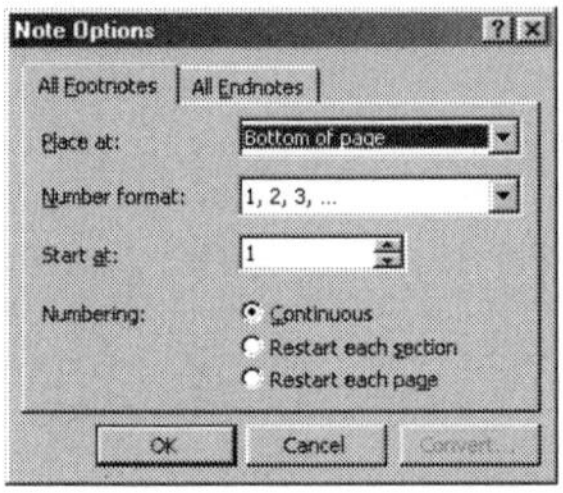

1. Click either the All Footnotes tab or the All Endnotes tab to tell Word which type of note you're going to experiment with. Both tab options look and work just about the same, by the way.
2. Select a position from the Place At drop-down list box to tell Word where notes should be placed. You have different options for footnotes and endnotes, and all the placement options are self-explanatory.
3. Select a numbering scheme from the Number Format drop-down list box. You can choose regular arabic numbers (1, 2, 3, . . .), roman numerals (i, ii, iii, . . .), alphabetic lettering (a, b, c, . . .), or symbols (*, †, ‡, . . .).
4. Enter a number in the Start At box to tell Word which footnote or endnote number to use first.
5. Select Numbering option buttons to tell Word whether and where it should restart the numbering.

Footnotes and Endnotes

You can add footnotes and endnotes to Word documents. A footnote appears at the bottom of the page. An endnote appears at the end of the **document.**

Adding Footnotes and Endnotes

To add footnotes and endnotes, follow these steps:

1 Move the **insertion point** to the place in your text where the footnote or endnote marker should be placed. (The marker is probably the footnote or endnote number.)

2 Choose the Insert menu's Footnote command.

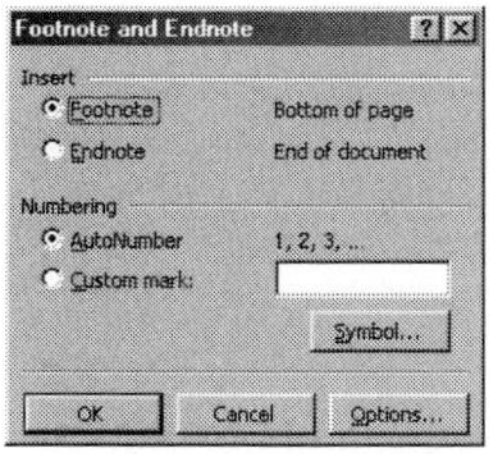

3 Select the Insert option buttons—Footnote and Endnote—to tell Word whether you want the note to appear at the foot of the page as a footnote or at the end of the document or document section as an endnote.

4 Select the Numbering option buttons to specify how footnotes should be marked. Click AutoNumber if they should be numbered (which is usually the case). Or if you want to use some other character (such as an asterisk), type the character in the Custom Mark text box.

5 Press Enter or click OK when you've finished selecting options in the Insert Footnote dialog box. If Word is in Normal view, it opens the Footnote pane and moves the insertion point to it so that you can type your footnote. If Word is in Print Layout view, the insertion point will appear at the proper footnote position.

Deleting Footnotes and Endnotes

To delete a footnote or an endnote, select the footnote or endnote marker. (The marker is probably the note number, unless you have assigned a custom note marker.) Then press Delete.

Note that when you delete a footnote or an endnote and you've used default numbering, Word renumbers the remaining document footnotes or endnotes after the deletion.

SEE ALSO **Footnote and Endnote Options**

Format Painting SEE Copying Formatting

Formatting

Automatic formatting SEE **AutoFormat**

Borders SEE **Paragraph Borders**

Changing character font and point size SEE **Changing Fonts**

Changing character spacing SEE **Character Spacing**

Creating format combinations SEE **Creating Styles**

Horizontal alignment SEE **Indentation and Alignment**

Page margins SEE **Margins**

Pagination and paragraphs SEE **Line And Page Breaks**

Replacing styles SEE **Changing Styles**

Searching for formatting SEE **Finding Formatting**

Shading SEE **Paragraph Borders; Coloring Documents**

Spacing SEE **Paragraph and Line Spacing**

Text around pictures SEE **Text Boxes**

Form Letters SEE Mail Merge

Formula Functions

Functions are prefabricated **formulas.** In Word, you can use functions in your table formulas.

Using Functions in Formulas

To use a function, first select the table cell in which you want to place the formula. Then choose the Table menu's Formula command. When Word displays the Formula dialog box, use the Paste Function box to select the function you want to use and the Number Format box to specify a format for the formula results. If the function requires or accepts multiple values, separate the values by using commas.

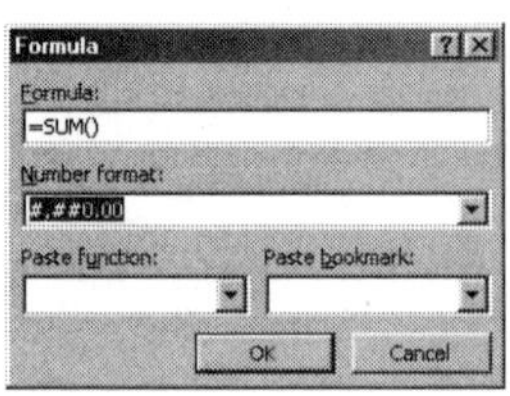

Reviewing Word's Functions

Word provides 18 functions, as shown in the following table:

Function	Purpose
ABS	Returns the absolute value of the input. For example, the function =ABS(-3) returns 3.
AND	Lets you perform a compound "AND" logic test. For example, the function =AND(1=1,2+2=4) returns 1 because both logical tests are true.
AVERAGE	Calculates the arithmetic mean, or average, of the input values. For example, the function =AVERAGE(1,2,3,4) returns 2.5.
COUNT	Counts the input values. For example, the function =COUNT(1,2,3,4,5,6) returns 6.
DEFINED	Determines whether a formula can be calculated, returning 1 if the formula can be calculated and 0 if it can't. For example, the function =DEFINED(1/0) returns 0 because you can't divide any number by 0.
FALSE	Returns the logical value for false, which is 0. For example, =FALSE returns 0.
IF	Performs a logical test and returns one result if the test is true and another if the test is false. For example, =IF(2+2=4,1,0) returns the value 1, proving once and for all that 2+2 does indeed equal 4.
INT	Returns the integer portion of a value. For example, =INT(3.5) returns 3.
MAX	Returns the largest input value. For example, the function =MAX(1,2,3,4) returns 4.
MIN	Returns the smallest input value. For example, the function =MIN(1,2,3,4) returns 1.
MOD	Returns the modulus, or remainder, left over from a division operation. For example, the function =MOD(3,2) returns 1 because that's what gets left over when you divide 3 by 2.
NOT	Lets you perform a compound "NOT" logic test. For example, the function =NOT(1=1,2+2=4) returns 0 because both logical tests are true.

continues

Formula Functions *(continued)*

Function	Purpose
OR	Lets you perform a compound "OR" logic test. For example, the function =OR(1>1,2+2=4) returns 1 because the second logical test is true.
PRODUCT	Multiplies the function arguments by each other. For example, =PRODUCT(2,3,4) returns 24.
ROUND	Rounds an input value to a specified decimal precision. For example, =ROUND(123.456,2) returns 123.46.
SIGN	Returns -1 if the input value is a negative value, a 1 if the input value is a positive value, or 0 if the input value is 0. For example, =SIGN(-3) returns -1.
SUM	Sums the input values. For example, =SUM(2,2) returns 4.
TRUE	Returns the logical value for true, 1. For example, =TRUE returns 1.

Word functions closely resemble Excel functions

Word formula functions work like a spreadsheet's functions. If you've used Microsoft Excel functions, you'll find using the Word functions easy and straightforward. Note, however, that you may not want to use Word formulas if you have Excel. You can easily create worksheet **objects** in Excel and then copy and paste them into Word documents.

Formulas

You can use formulas in the **cells** of a table. The table shown below, for example, shows an example travel budget. Each of the values shown in the table is calculated using a formula. The Hotel cost estimate, for example, is calculated using the formula ={8*175}, and the Airfare cost estimate is calculated using the formula ={4*250}.

Hotel	1400
Airfare	1000
Meals	1440
Total	3840

Writing Your Own Formulas

To write a formula for a table cell, select the cell. Then choose the Table menu's Formula command. When Word displays the Formula dialog box, type the formula. Begin the formula with the = sign, and use the arithmetic operators + for addition, - for subtraction, * for multiplication, / for division, and ^ for exponentiation. Override standard arithmetic operator precedence rules by using parentheses. When you press Enter or click OK, Word places the formula in the cell, calculating the formula result.

If you want to see the formula rather than the formula result, right-click the cell and then choose the Toggle Field Codes command.

Note that you don't type the { } braces. Word adds them for you. Word uses braces to identify field codes.

Using Cell Addresses

You can use table cell addresses in a formula, in which case Word uses the value in the referenced cell. Table cell addresses consist of the column letter and the row number. Table columns are lettered A, B, C, and so on. Table rows are numbered 1, 2, 3, and so on. So table cell A1 is the cell in the upper left corner of the table.

Adding AutoSum Formulas

Word supplies several formula functions that you can use in table formulas, too. One of the most useful is the AutoSum function. To use AutoSum, select the cell where the total formula should be entered, and choose the Table menu's Formula command. Word automatically writes the formula {=SUM(ABOVE)}, which totals the cells in a table. To use this formula, click OK.

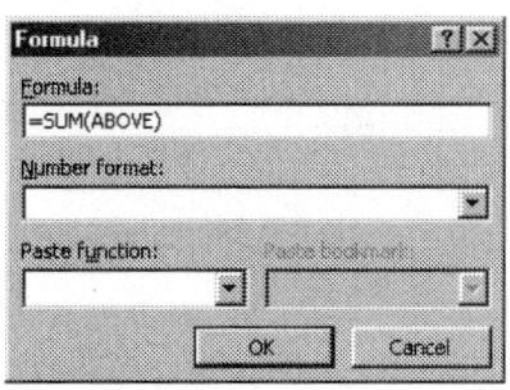

Recalculating Formulas Because Inputs Change

You can recalculate a table formula when an input to the formula changes. Select the cell with the formula, and then press F9. Or right-click the cell with the formula, and then choose the shortcut menu's Update Field command.

continues

Formulas *(continued)*

Note, however, that Word recalculates only the formula you select—and not those that depend on the formula. For example, look at the table on page 66, which shows travel costs. If you change the Hotel cost estimate by changing that cell's formula, selecting the cell and pressing F9 causes Word to update only the Hotel cost estimate value. To update the Total cost estimate, you need to also select that cell and press F9 again.

To recalculate all the formulas in a table, first select the entire table by choosing the Table menu's Select command and then choosing the submenu's Table command. Then press F9.

More on formulas

You can also use prefabricated **formula functions** by selecting a function from the Paste Function list box.

Fractions

You can enter fractional characters—¼, ½, and ¾, for example—in documents. You can also create reasonable-looking fractions by using numbers and the Slash key. If you type 1/2 or 1/4, the Word AutoFormat feature changes them into ½ and ¼ (unless you tell it not to). You can also tell AutoCorrect to make that change to other fractions you create from scratch. This method is faster than entering symbols if you often use specific fractions.

Using Fraction Symbols

To use a fractional character, choose the Insert menu's Symbol command, select Normal Text from the Font drop-down list box, and then click the fraction you want. When you use this command, your fraction is actually a single character.

Creating Fractions from Scratch

You can also create a reasonable-looking fraction by reducing the point size of the numbers and the slash characters (as compared with what you're using elsewhere in the document), by making the numerator a superscript character and the denominator a subscript character, as in $^{3}/_{8}$. When you use the superscript-and-subscript approach, your fraction is actually a combination of smaller-than-normal characters.

SEE ALSO AutoCorrect; AutoFormat; Changing Fonts; Symbols

Frames

In Microsoft Word 2000, frames work like **web browser** frames. In essence, a frame is a document component that appears in its own **window pane.** A common use of frames is to create a table of contents frame that includes **hyperlinks** pointing to the parts of the main document frame. In this case, someone uses the table of contents frame to navigate the larger, main document. Note, then, that frames are really tools for making it easier to move within and organize documents, such as web pages, that will be viewed online.

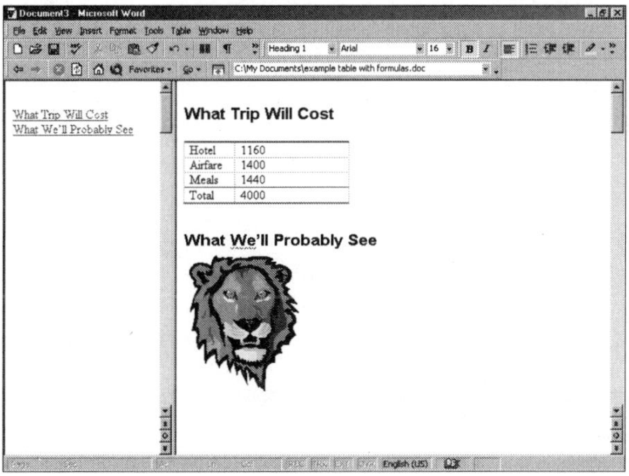

Adding a Table of Contents Frame

You can rather easily add a table of contents to a document that uses the Word standard heading styles. To do this, choose the Format menu's Frames command and then choose the submenu's Table Of Contents In Frame command. Word creates a new table of contents frame based on the document's headings. In the new table of contents frame, these headings are hyperlinks. If you click one of these hyperlinks, Word selects the corresponding heading in the main document frame.

Adding Another Frame

To add a frame, choose the Format menu's Frames command and then choose the New Frame command from the submenu. After you create the frame, you fill it with text and probably hyperlinks.

continues

Frames *(continued)*

After you've added a frame to a document, Word replaces the New Frame command with the New Frame Left, New Frame Right, New Frame Above, and New Frame Below commands. You use these commands to add frames in specific locations relative to the selected frame.

Customizing Frame Properties

When you add a frame to a document, Word adds a Frame Properties command to the Frame submenu. If you choose this command, Word displays the Frame Properties dialog box, which supplies two tabs: Frame and Borders. The Frame tab lets you do things like name the frame and set its size. The Borders tab lets you describe how the borders should appear—their size and color, for example.

SEE ALSO Text Boxes

Full Screen

You can use all of your screen to display a **document.** When you view a document as a full screen, Word displays only the document. Word doesn't display the menu bar, the **toolbars,** or the title bars of the **program window** and the **document window.**

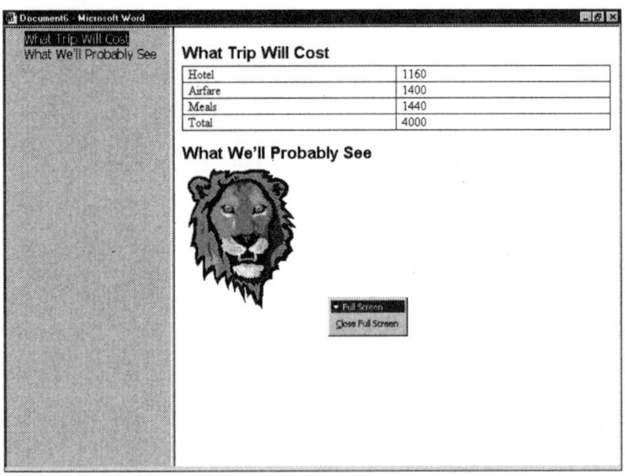

Viewing the Full Screen

To view the Word program window as a full screen, choose the View menu's Full Screen command.

Viewing the Regular Screen

To return to the regular view of the program window, click the Close Full Screen button that Word displays in the Full Screen view. Or press Esc.

Choosing commands when Word is in Full Screen view

Even though the menu bar doesn't show up when you're using Full Screen view in the Word program window, you can still choose menu commands. All you have to do is move the mouse pointer to the top of the screen, and the menu bar slides into view.

Functions SEE Formula Functions

Go To

You can use the Edit menu's Go To command to quickly move to some new location in a document. This command is particularly useful in large documents. To use the Go To command, follow these steps:

1 Choose the Edit menu's Go To command, or double-click in the left half of the status bar. Word displays the Go To tab of the Find And Replace dialog box.

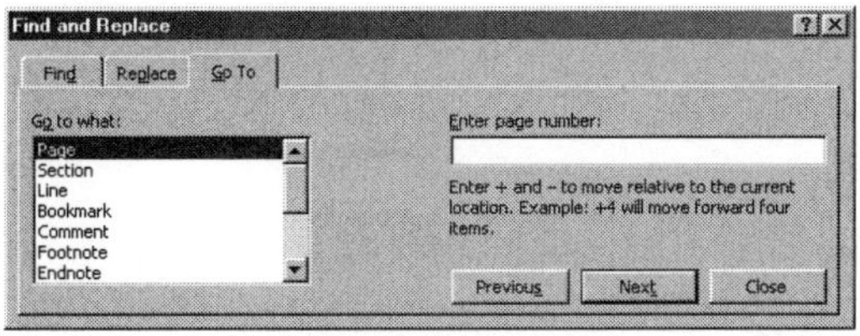

2 Select an option from the Go To What list box, and enter a number in the Enter Page Number text box to describe where you want the insertion point to move. As you select different document parts—pages, sections, lines, and bookmarks, for example—Word renames the text box to correspond to the selected entry.

Grammar Checking SEE Automatic Grammar Checking

Graphs

Word comes with the Microsoft Graph application. You use Graph to add charts to your Word **documents** and other Microsoft Office documents.

Describing the To-Be-Plotted Data

The easiest way to describe the data you want to plot in a graph is to create a **table** that holds the data. To do this, follow these steps:

1. Choose the Table menu's Insert Table command to add a table to the document.
2. Fill the table rows with descriptions of what you want to plot and with the data itself.

Sales	125	135	150	170
Profits	-5	5	10	20

Plotting Data

After you've created a table with the data you want to show in a graph, you're ready to chart the data. To do this, follow these steps:

1. Select the table by clicking a **cell.** Then choose the Table menu's Select command and the submenu's Table command.
2. Choose the Insert menu's Object command.
3. Click the Create New tab.
4. Select Microsoft Graph 2000 chart from the Object Type list box.
5. If you want to display an icon in the Word document, select the Display As Icon check box. (After Graph creates the chart and inserts the icon in the document, just click the icon to display the chart.)
6. Click OK. Word places the data in a Microsoft Graph datasheet and displays a chart of your data. If you want, you can change the data plotted in the chart by changing the data shown in the datasheet. Essentially, the datasheet works like a simple Microsoft Excel worksheet.

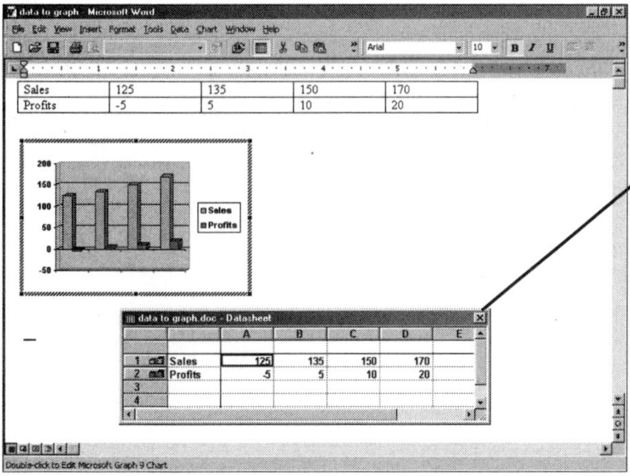

Close the datasheet window by clicking its Close button. You can reopen the datasheet window by clicking the chart.

Microsoft Graph uses two document windows

You'll see two document windows in the Graph application window: one shows the graph; the other, called a datasheet, shows the table. You can edit the table data by using the datasheet document window.

Moving the Legend

The legend, which identifies the data you've plotted, initially appears inside the plot area—usually on top of the chart. You can move it by clicking it (to select it) and then dragging it to a new location.

Choosing a Chart Type

Although Graph chooses an initial chart type for you—a three-dimensional column chart—you can easily select another chart type by choosing the Chart menu's Chart Type command. When you do, Graph shows pictures of the various chart types. You can pick a chart type simply by clicking it.

Adding, Moving, and Removing Chart Titles

To add text that describes a chart and its data, select the whole chart area and then right-click it. Choose the shortcut menu's Chart Options command. In the Chart Options dialog box, click the Titles tab and then type the title for the chart in the Chart Title box. If you want category, series, or value titles, type them in their respective text boxes. Then click OK.

continues

Graphs *(continued)*

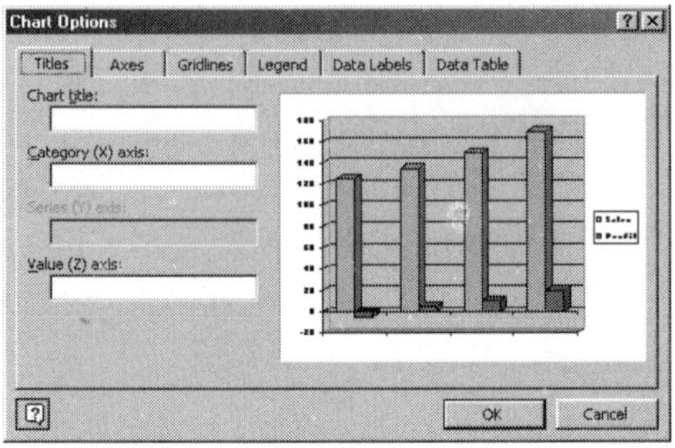

After you've added a title to a chart, you can move the text you add by selecting it and dragging.

You can remove a chart title by selecting it and pressing Delete.

Adding and Removing Data Labels

To label a chart's markers with the plotted values or percentages, select the chart, right-click it, and choose the shortcut menu's Chart Options command. Click the Data Labels tab, click the appropriate option button, and then click OK. (In general, you add only percentage labels to pie charts.)

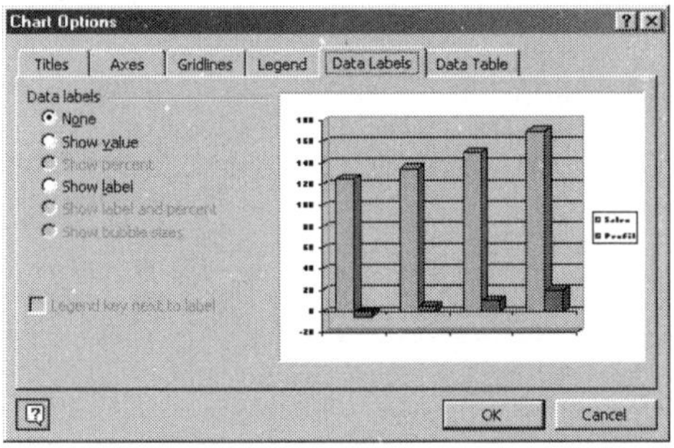

You can remove data labels by clicking them and then pressing Delete.

Adding and Removing Legends

A legend identifies the data you've plotted. You can remove a legend by selecting the legend and then pressing Delete. Or if a chart doesn't already have a legend, you can add one by choosing the Chart menu's Chart Options command, clicking the Legend tab, and then selecting the Show Legend check box.

Legend names

If you organize your to-be-plotted data into rows, Graph uses the contents of the first cell in the row to name the data in the legend.

Adding and Removing Axes

If you don't need axes to calibrate the plotted data, you can remove the axes by selecting the chart, right-clicking it, and choosing the shortcut menu's Chart Options command. Click the Axes tab, and select check boxes and options to turn on and off the display of vertical, horizontal, and—in the case of a three-dimensional chart—depth axes.

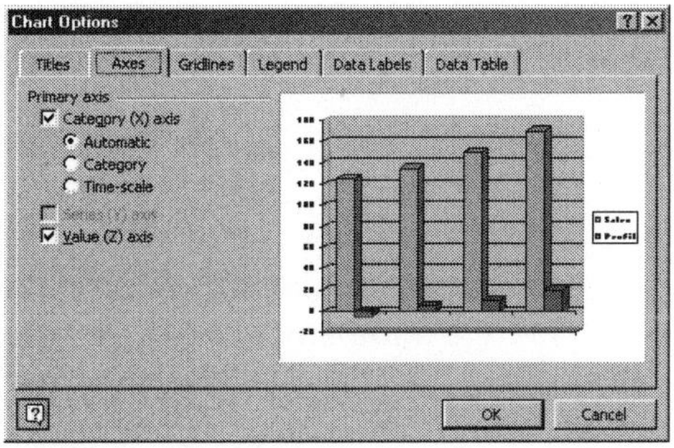

Adding and Removing Gridlines

Graph will add vertical and horizontal gridlines to the plot area. Sometimes these gridlines make it easier for readers to understand the chart markers. Just select the chart, right-click it, and choose the shortcut menu's Chart Options command. Click the Gridlines tab, and select or clear the check boxes to turn on and turn off the display of vertical and horizontal gridlines.

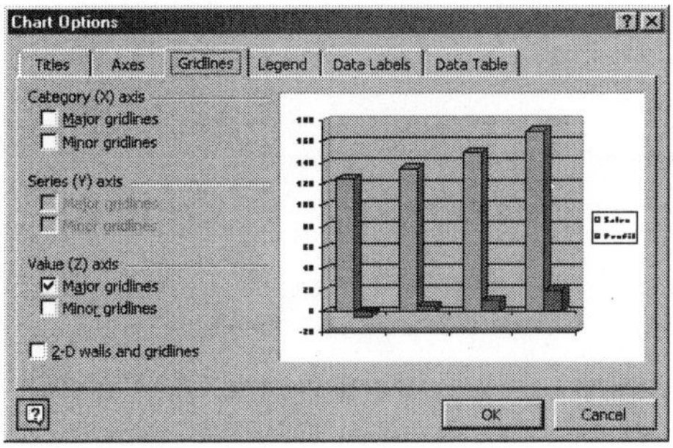

continues

Graphs *(continued)*

Formatting the Chart

The Format menu provides a series of commands you can use to change the way the parts of your chart look. In general, you format a chart by double-clicking the chart part you want to change and then using the dialog box Graph displays to make your changes.

Returning to the Word Document

After you finish choosing a chart type and making any other changes to the graph, click another part of the document. Graph closes. You return to your Word document, which will now show the new chart.

SEE ALSO Creating Tables; Embedding New Objects; Tables

Headers and Footers

Headers and footers appear in the top and bottom margins of pages and usually describe some aspect of the printed page or document—for example, the page number.

You can use a different header or footer for the first page in a document, for odd- and even-numbered pages, and in each different document section.

Adding a Header or a Footer

Choose the View menu's Header And Footer command. Word changes the document view to show laid-out pages. It also draws a dashed line in the top or bottom margin of the page to show where the header or footer will be placed and displays the Header And Footer toolbar.

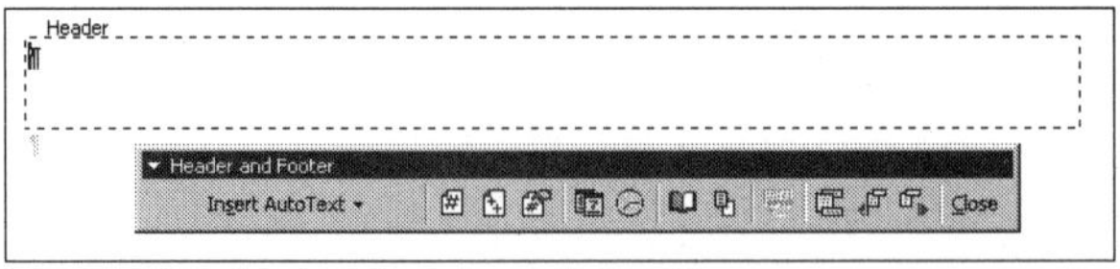

You can type whatever you want in the Header box or Footer box.

Using the Header And Footer Toolbar

You can also use the Header And Footer toolbar to build your headers and footers:

Tool	Description
	Adds an AutoText entry to a header or footer.
	Adds a page number to a header or footer.
	Adds the total number of pages in the document to a header or footer.
	Displays the Page Number Format dialog box.
	Adds a date to a header or footer.
	Adds the current system time to a header or footer.
	Displays the Page Setup dialog box.
	Hides and unhides the document text.
	Tells Word to make this page's header or footer the same as the previous one.
	Toggles between the page's header and footer.
	Shows the previous page's header or footer.
	Shows the next page's header or footer.
	Closes the Header box or Footer box and removes the toolbar.

SEE ALSO **Document Views**

Help

If you need help with a task, choose the Help menu's What's This? command (or press Shift+F1). Word adds a question mark to the mouse pointer.

Then click any menu command, toolbar button, or part of a window (other than text) that you need help with. The Help application displays specific information about what you selected.

Highlighting Text

If you like to underline or highlight favorite passages in books, Word has a tool for marking passages in documents. It's the Highlight toolbar button. To use this tool, click the down arrow to the right of it and then select a color from the drop-down list box. The mouse pointer changes to a pen. Drag the pointer over the text you want to highlight. When you finish, click the Highlight toolbar button again to turn it off.

History

Word maintains a history of the documents you've opened. You can view this history from either the File menu's Open or Save As dialog boxes by clicking the History shortcut.

HTML

HTML, an acronym, stands for hypertext markup language. HTML is essentially the language the Internet uses for **web pages.** When your **web browser** displays a web page, for example, what you're really viewing is an HTML document.

HTML is also relevant to Microsoft Office 2000. The Office 2000 programs, including Word, let you save your documents by using the traditional binary file format, which previous editions used. But you can also save your documents by using the HTML file format. One big benefit of using the HTML file format is that many (although not all) web browsers will be able to view the contents of Office documents that use the HTML file format.

SEE ALSO Saving Web Pages

Hyperlink

You can put a link to basically any Internet resource—including **World Wide Web** pages—or local network resource in your **documents.** You can also make a hyperlink to another Word document on your system or network, or even to another location in the active document.

Inserting a Hyperlink

To insert a hyperlink, follow these steps:

1 Select your **insertion point**.

2 Choose the Insert menu's Hyperlink command. Or click the Insert Hyperlink toolbar button.

Enter the URL or file pathname in the Type The File Or Web Page Name text box.

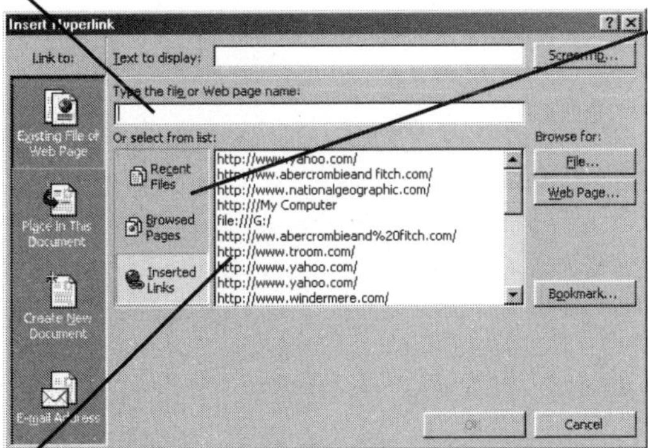

If you don't know the URL or file pathname but you have recently opened the web page or file or used it in another hyperlink, click the Recent Files, Browsed Pages, or Inserted Links shortcut.

Select the URL or file pathname from the list box.

3 If you want the hyperlink to point to a web page or file you already know the location of, click the Existing File Or Web Page shortcut.

Using the Browse For buttons

If you click the Existing File Or Web Page shortcut, you can then click the Browse For File button to open a dialog box you can use to locate a file you can't find some other way. And you can click the Browse For Web Page button to start Microsoft Internet Explorer, which you can use to locate a web page you can't find some other way.

continues

Hyperlink *(continued)*

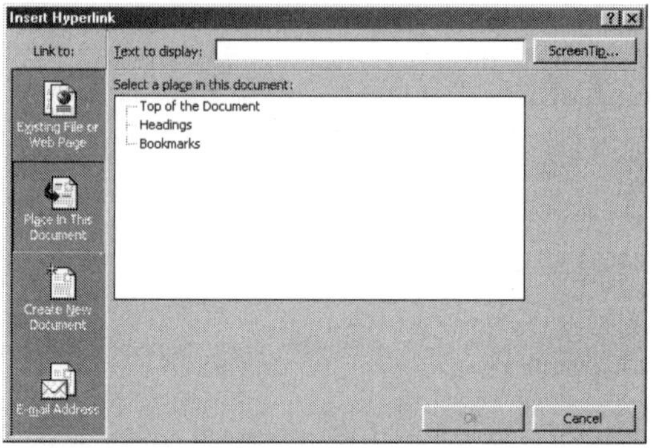

4 If you want the hyperlink to point to some location in the active document, click the Place In This Document shortcut. Then select from the available choices.

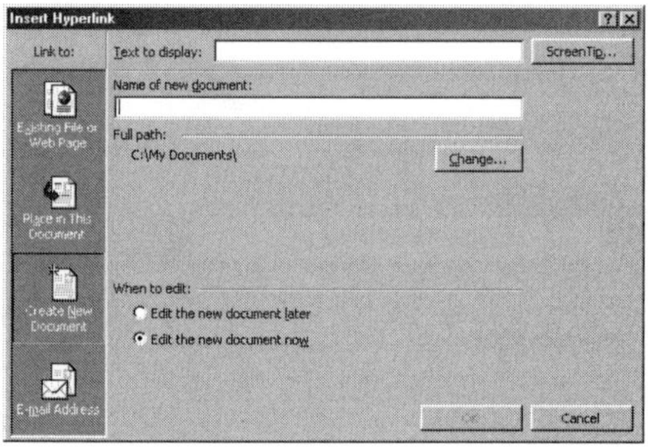

5 If you want the hyperlink to point to a new document you need to create, click the Create New Document shortcut. Then enter the document's full pathname in the Name Of New Document text box. Click the When To Edit buttons to indicate whether you want to begin working with the document immediately or later on.

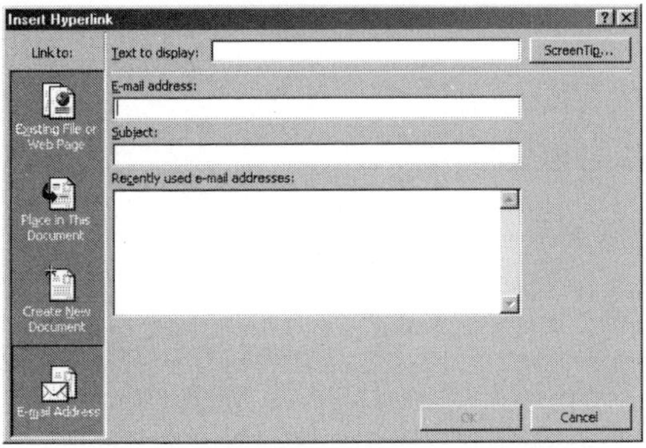

6 If you want the hyperlink to point to an e-mail address, click the E-Mail Address shortcut. Then enter the person's full e-mail address in the E-Mail Address text box. Enter a brief subject in the Subject text box to provide a subject line for the e-mail messages that will be sent when someone clicks this hyperlink. If you don't know the person's e-mail address, you may be able to select the e-mail address from the Recently Used E-Mail Addresses list box.

7 Click OK to add the hyperlink.

Using the Hyperlink

After you've inserted a hyperlink, the pointer changes to a hand when it's positioned over the cell containing the hyperlink. Click to open the linked web page. To edit the hyperlink, right-click it and then choose the shortcut menu's Edit Hyperlink command.

Hyphenation

You can use hyphens to minimize the raggedness of the right margin. Choose the Tools menu's Language command, and then choose the submenu's Hyphenation command.

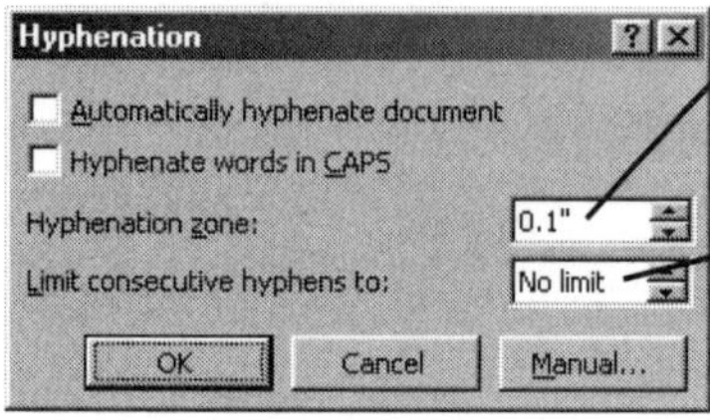

The Hyphenation Zone box specifies how close to the edge of the right margin words can end.

The Limit Consecutive Hyphens To box tells Word how many lines in a row can end with hyphens.

Suppressing hyphenation

You can tell Word that it shouldn't hyphenate words in the selected paragraph. To do this, choose the Format menu's Paragraph command, click the Line And Page Breaks tab, and select the Don't Hyphenate check box.

Importing Documents

You can open documents created by other word-processing programs. You can also import any ASCII text file. To do this, choose the File menu's Open command. Identify the format of the file to be imported in the Files Of Type drop-down list box. Specify the file's location in the Look In text box. Type the name of the file in the File Name drop-down list box, or select the file from the list. Then click Open.

Indentation and Alignment

You can change paragraph indenting and alignment by choosing the Format menu's Paragraph command. An indent is the space between the margin edge and the spot where a line of text starts or must end. Paragraph alignment refers to how the lines of text appear between the left and right margins.

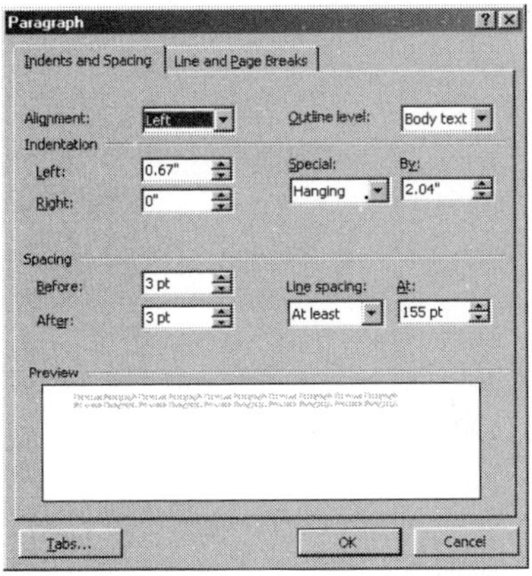

1. Select an option from the Alignment box to specify whether the paragraph should be aligned Left, Right, Centered, or Justified (aligned left and right).
2. Select an option from the Outline Level box to specify the level on the outline, if any.
3. Enter an amount in the Left and Right boxes to specify indentation in inches.
4. Specify special indentation in the Special and By boxes.

SEE ALSO **Paragraph and Line Spacing**

Index

An index is simply an alphabetized list of the terms used in a document. An index can be a handy tool for readers. (That's why we put one in this book, for example.) You can add indexes to your documents.

Adding an index is a two-part process. The first part of the process is telling Word which terms belong in your index. The second part of the process is telling Word to build the index by using the terms you selected.

Adding Index Entries

1. Select a term.
2. Choose the Insert menu's Index And Tables command.
3. On the Index tab, click Mark Entry. Word displays the Mark Index Entry dialog box.

continues

Index *(continued)*

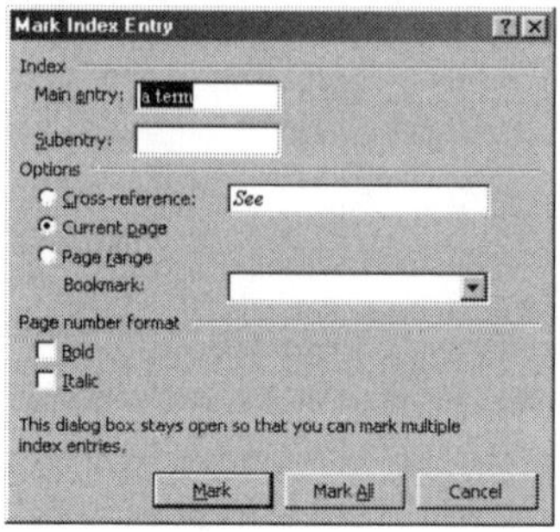

4 Click Mark.

5 Word leaves the Mark Index Entry dialog box open. You can add additional terms to your index by scrolling through your document, selecting terms, opening the dialog box, and then clicking Mark.

Index field codes

As you mark each index entry, Word adds the index entry field code following the word. If you tell Word to add the term *Document* to your index, it adds the field code {XE "Document"} to your document. You'll see this code if the Show/Hide ¶ toolbar button is selected. (Marking an entry turns on the Show/Hide ¶ toolbar button automatically.)

Building the Index

1 Place the insertion point where you want the index to be generated, and then choose the Insert menu's Index And Tables command.

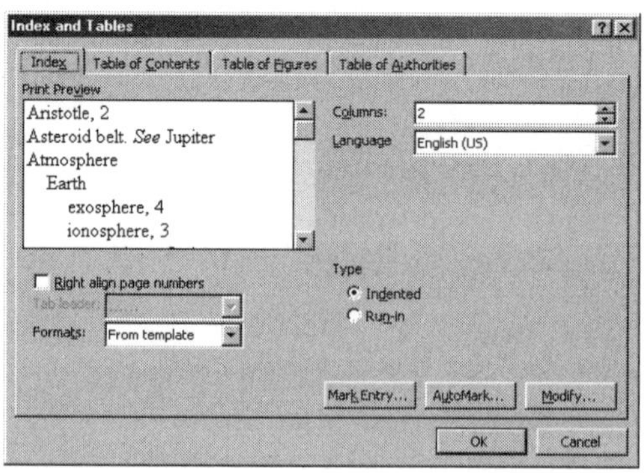

2 Click the Index tab if it isn't already displayed.

3. Choose a type and a format for your index. The Print Preview box shows what the index will look like with the choices you've made.
4. Click OK to generate the index. Word will look through your document, finding each of the index entry field codes. Whenever Word finds one, it will add the term to your index and indicate the page number.

About indexes

There's more to the mechanics of index creation than I've described here. What's more, good indexing is an art. Therefore, if you get into this indexing business, let me offer a couple of suggestions. First, consider reviewing the discussion of indexing in the Word user documentation. Or get a tutorial that covers indexing in painstaking detail. Second, start looking at the indexes in books like this one. You can learn a great deal by reviewing the work of a professional indexer (such as the woman who indexed this book).

Insertion Point

The insertion point is the blinking vertical bar that shows you where what you type gets placed. To see it, start Word, begin typing, and look at the bar that moves ahead of the text you type. That's the insertion point.

Installing Word

Microsoft Office 2000 is very smart about the way it installs Word and the other Office programs on your computer. For example, the Office setup program looks at your computer and any previous installations before it installs Word, in order to install only the parts of Word you're likely to use. Also, if some piece of the Word program becomes damaged or necessary, Word will automatically repair itself by reinstalling damaged components or installing missing components. For these reasons, you may occasionally find yourself prompted to supply the Office CD or Word CD.

Italic Characters

To *italicize* **characters,** select them and then either press Ctrl+I or click the Italic toolbar button. You can also choose the Format menu's Font command.

Justify SEE Right-Justify

Kerning SEE Character Spacing

Laptop Computers

If you're using Word on a laptop computer, you should know that almost everything described in this book applies with equal measure to your computing environment. You should also consider two other, minor points. First, because pointing devices on a laptop are often challenging to use, remember that everything you want to do can also be accomplished with your keyboard. You can activate the menu bar, for example, by pressing Alt. After you've done this, you can select menus and commands by pressing the underlined letter or number in their name.

A second point to remember if you're using a laptop is that some of the Word installation features won't work on your laptop unless you have access to the original Word installation information—such as the original installation CD. As described in the **Installing Word** and **Detect And Repair** entries, Word may need to install additional components of the program as you work or may need to repair damaged components of the program.

Letter Wizard

What if your computer got so smart that it could write all your letters and memos for you? It hasn't happened yet, but Word's Letter Wizard comes close. Maybe you want organized, well-written examples of specific kinds of correspondence you can adapt to suit your needs, or maybe you would rather compose your own text from scratch but would like to never worry about nitpicky formatting. Either way, the Word Letter Wizard gives you as much or as little assistance as you want. To use the Letter Wizard, follow the steps on the next page:

1 Choose the Tools menu's Letter Wizard command.

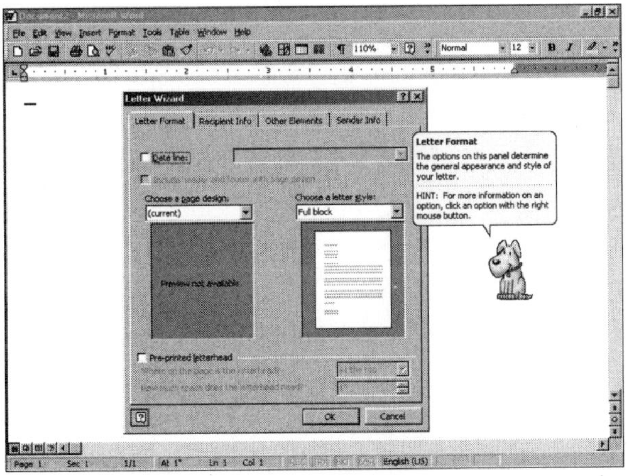

2 In the Letter Format tab of the Letter Wizard dialog box, select the Date Line check box if you want to add the date. Select a format for the date in the drop-down list to the right.

3 Select the type of correspondence you want from the Choose A Page Design list box. Look at the preview box to see its appearance. If the design has a header or a footer, the Include Header And Footer With Page Design check box becomes active. Select this check box to include the design's header or footer.

4 Select a style (for example, Full Block, Modified Block, or Semi-Block) in the Choose A Letter Style list box.

5 If you plan to print the letter or memo on letterhead, select the Pre-Printed Letterhead check box. This step activates list boxes where you tell Word the position of the letterhead design and how much space Word needs to leave blank for it.

6 Click the Recipient Info tab, and type or select the name of the recipient of the letter and the recipient's address if it is not automatically displayed when you select a name. Or use the Address Book toolbar button to find a name and address you've listed in your Address Book.

Starting the Letter Wizard

If the Office Assistant sees that you've begun to write a letter, it offers to help by starting the Letter Wizard. To start the Letter Wizard, click Get Help With Writing The Letter. If you don't want assistance, click the Office Assistant's Just Type The Letter Without Help button. Note that you can also start the Letter Wizard by choosing the File menu's New command, clicking the Letters And Faxes tab, and then double-clicking the Letter Wizard icon.

continues

Letter Wizard *(continued)*

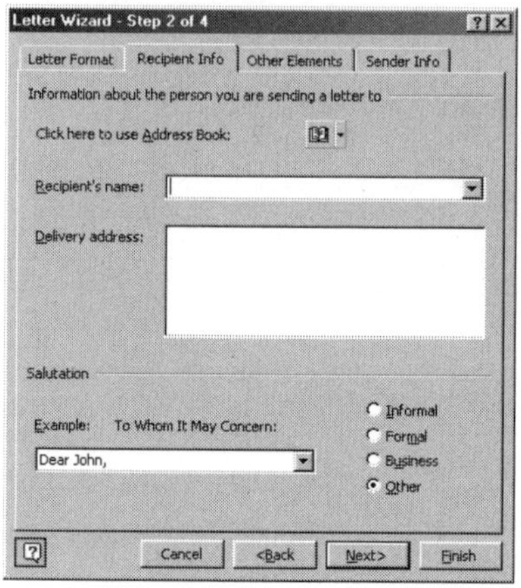

7 Click an option button in the Salutation area to choose a formal, businesslike, or not-so-formal salutation.

8 Click the Other Elements tab to include a reference line, mailing instructions, attention line, or subject line and to tell Word to whom to send a carbon copy, if applicable.

9 Click the Sender Info tab, and type or select the sender's name and the sender's address if it is not automatically displayed when you select a name. Or use the Address Book toolbar button instead. To omit the return address, select the Omit check box.

10 In the Closing area, select or type a complimentary closing, a job title, a company name, writer/typist initials, and the number of enclosures, or leave any of these boxes blank.

11 Click Next (if that button is displayed). Or click the other tabs of the Letter Wizard dialog box. When Word displays the other tabs of the dialog box, use their boxes and buttons to collect the other pieces of information you'll want to add to the letter.

12 When you finish filling in the Letter Wizard's boxes and clicking its buttons, click Finish. Word adds any information appropriate to your letter and also appropriate **styles** you can use to format elements of the letter.

SEE ALSO Applying Styles

Line And Page Breaks

You can use the Word Line And Page Breaks settings to control how Word breaks **paragraphs** between pages, how it hyphenates, and how it numbers the lines in a **document.** To perform this sort of controlled text flow, select the text for which you want to specify line and page breaks and then follow these steps:

1 Choose the Format menu's Paragraph command, and then click the Line And Page Breaks tab.

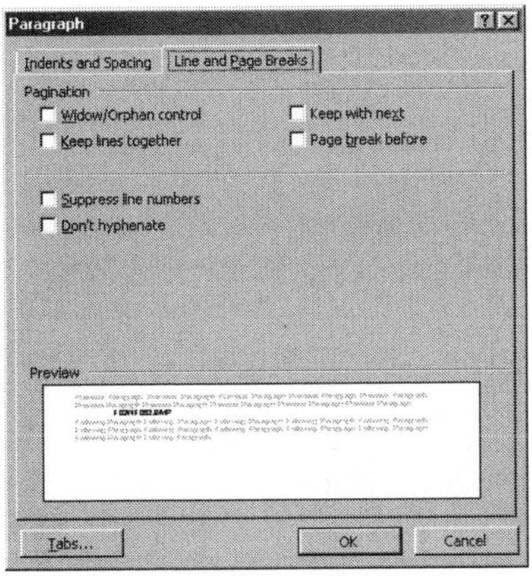

2 Select the Widow/Orphan Control check box to tell Word not to print the first or last line of a paragraph on a separate page.

3 Select the Keep With Next check box to tell Word not to break pages between the selected paragraph and the next paragraph.

4 Select the Keep Lines Together check box to tell Word not to break the selected paragraph between pages.

5 Select the Page Break Before check box to tell Word to start this paragraph on a new page. Use the Preview box to see roughly how your text-flow control settings work.

6 Select the Suppress Line Numbers check box to tell Word that it shouldn't print the **line numbers** you've added to the document.

7 Select the Don't Hyphenate check box if you don't want Word to use **hyphenation.**

SEE ALSO Orphan; Widow

Line Numbers

You can number the lines in a document **section.** To do this, choose the File menu's Page Setup command, click the Layout tab, click Line Numbers, and then select the Add Line Numbering check box.

Suppressing line numbers

You can format a paragraph so that it doesn't show line numbers even if you've told Word to number all the lines in a document section. To do this, select the paragraph and choose the Format menu's Paragraph command. Then click the Line And Page Breaks tab, and select the Suppress Line Numbers check box.

Line Spacing SEE Paragraph and Line Spacing

Macro

A macro is simply a series of commands, which means that a macro is really a simple program. Macros are very handy because they let you automate tasks within Word. For example, if you continually repeat some action numerous times, writing a macro that automates the action may be simpler.

Recording a Macro

The easiest way to write a macro is to tell Word that it should record the sequence of steps you want to automate. To do this, follow these steps:

1 Choose the Tools menu's Macro command, and then choose the submenu's Record New Macro command. Word displays the Record Macro dialog box.

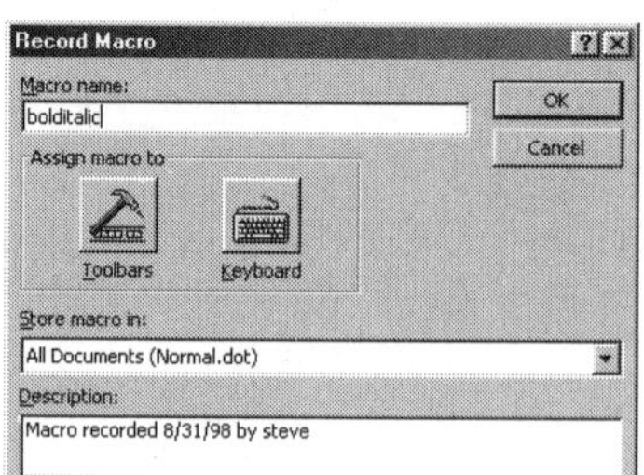

2 Enter a self-descriptive name for the macro in the Macro Name text box.

3 Optionally, use either the Toolbars or Keyboard button to assign the macro to a toolbar button or keyboard combination. You do this so that you can run the macro by clicking the toolbar button or by pressing the keyboard combination. When you click either Toolbars or Keyboard, Word displays another dialog box you use to identify the toolbar button or provide the keyboard combination.

4 Select a location from the Store Macro In drop-down list box to indicate in which Word document or template the macro should be stored. Typically, you'll store the macro in either a specific word document where the macro will be used or the normal.dot **template,** which is the document template on which most new documents are based.

5 Click OK. Word closes the Record Macro dialog box and displays the Macro toolbar, which provides two buttons: Stop Recording and Pause Recording. Click Stop Recording to tell Word when it should stop recording your actions. Click Pause Recording to tell Word that it should temporarily pause its recording of your actions. To "unpause" your actions, click Pause Recording again.

6 Perform the exact sequence of actions you want Word to record.

7 Click the Macro toolbar's Stop button.

Writing a Macro from Scratch

You can write macros from scratch by using the Microsoft **Visual Basic** for Applications programming language. Note, however, that Visual Basic programming, although not overly difficult, is more involved than most Word users will have time for. To comfortably program in Visual Basic, you should learn about both structured programming and the Visual Basic development environment.

Running a Macro

You run a macro in three ways. If you've created a toolbar for the macro, you can run the macro by clicking the button. If you've created a shortcut key combination for the macro, you can run the macro by pressing the keyboard combination you specified as the shortcut. You can also run a macro by choosing the Tools menu's Macro command and then choosing the submenu's Macros command. When Word displays the Macros dialog box, double-click the macro you want to run.

Macro Viruses

Macro viruses are contained in objects saved in documents that can execute commands. **Macros,** toolbars, menus, and shortcuts are all in this category. Most objects in documents are harmless, of course, but if you open Word documents from sources you don't know and trust (download from the Internet, for example), or from sites that tend to have problems with viruses (like campus computer labs), you may open a document with an object that contains a macro virus. Fortunately, Word warns you when you attempt to open a document that could contain a macro virus.

SEE ALSO Virus

Mail Merge

Word can produce form letters, mailing labels, and other similar documents by extracting information from a database of names and addresses and then using this information to "fill in the blanks" in a standard document.

Creating the Main Mail Merge Document

Creating a special merge document, is a very simple procedure. To do so, follow these steps:

1. Choose the Tools menu's Mail Merge command. Word displays the Mail Merge Helper dialog box.

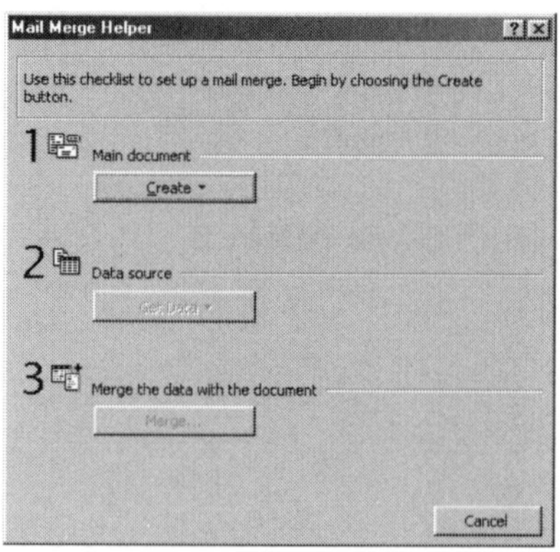

2. Click Create. Word displays a menu that lists mail merge document types: form letters, mailing labels, envelopes, and catalogs.

3 Choose an option, such as Form Letters.

4 When Word asks, indicate whether you want to make the active document a mail merge document or create a new, blank mail merge document.

Your next task is to identify the database that will supply the information used to create the mail merge document.

Creating Your Mail Merge Database in Word

1 If the Word program doesn't already display the Mail Merge Helper dialog box, choose the Tools menu's Mail Merge command.

2 Click Get Data.

3 When Word displays a menu of data source options, choose Create Data Source. Word displays the Create Data Source dialog box.

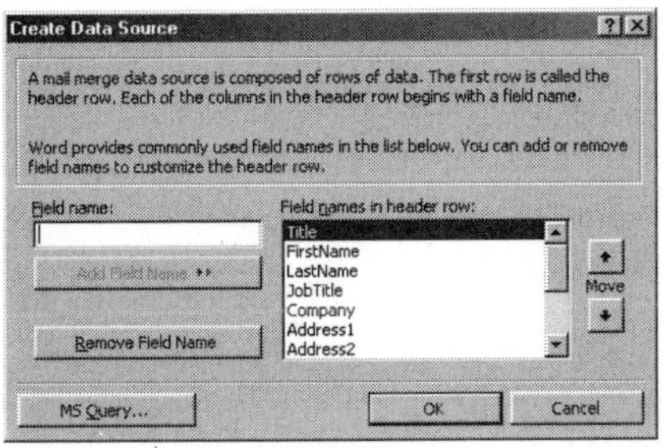

4 Remove fields you don't need from the Field Names In Header Row list box by selecting them and then clicking Remove Field Name.

5 Add fields you do need but that aren't already in the Field Names In Header Row list box by typing a field name in the Field Name text box and then clicking Add Field Name.

6 Click OK. Word displays the Save As dialog box. Use it to give a name to the database file. (Word database files are simply document files with tables.)

Mailing lists

Word assumes that you want to build a mailing list **database,** and it lists fields appropriate for this type of database. The fields, by the way, are simply the individual blocks of information that are stored for each entry, or record, in the database. In a database that lists names and addresses, each person's name and address represents a record. The fields, or information blocks, might include the person's title, first name, middle initial, last name, street address, city, and state.

7 Name the file, and select a location. (This step works the same way as naming a regular document file and selecting its location.)

continues

Mail Merge *(continued)*

8 When Word asks whether you want to add records to the database, indicate that you do by clicking Edit Data Source. Word displays the Data Form dialog box.

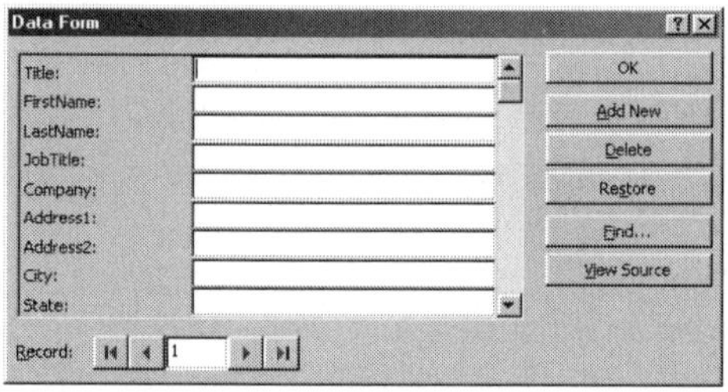

9 Enter records into your database by filling in the text boxes and then clicking Add New. Enter record numbers in the Record box or click the arrows to move backward and forward in the database. If you enter a record by mistake, display it and then click Delete. If you enter some bit of wrong information, display the record, fix the mistake, and move to the next record. When you finish with this step, click OK.

Using an External Database for Mail Merges

You don't have to create a database from scratch if one already exists. To use an existing external database, follow these steps:

1 Choose the Tools menu's Mail Merge command. Word displays the Mail Merge Helper dialog box.

2 Click Get Data.

3 When Word displays a list box of data source options, select Open Data Source. Word displays the Open Data Source dialog box.

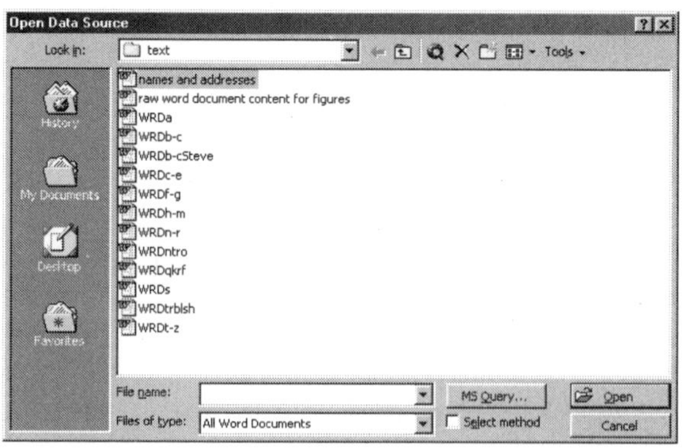

4 Select the filename, and specify its location. Then click Open.

Using different file types

Note that you may need to supply the file extension if it's something other than DOC. If you want to open a Microsoft Excel database, for example, which is actually called a list, you need to indicate the XLS file extension. You can open the List Files Of Type drop-down list box to see a list of the file formats you can use as data sources.

Describing and Writing the Main Mail Merge Document

After you've created the main mail merge document and either created or opened the data source, you're ready to specify how the main mail merge document should look.

To create the body text, simply type it in. The only unique feature of using a mail merge document is that you need to tell Word where the database record's fields should get placed. For example, if you've stored a person's name and address, you probably want these pieces of information to appear in an address block at the beginning of the letter.

To place a database record field in the document, position the insertion point, click the Insert Merge Field toolbar button so that Word displays a list of the database record fields, and select the field.

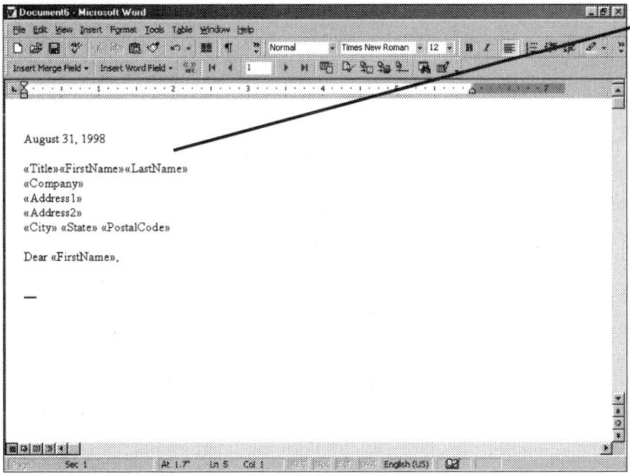

Word adds a field code (which simply names the database record field) to the document, as shown in the illustration.

continues

Mail Merge *(continued)*

Running a Mail Merge

After you've created the mail merge document, created or opened a data source, and described how the mail merge document should look, you're ready to run the merge. To do this, follow these steps:

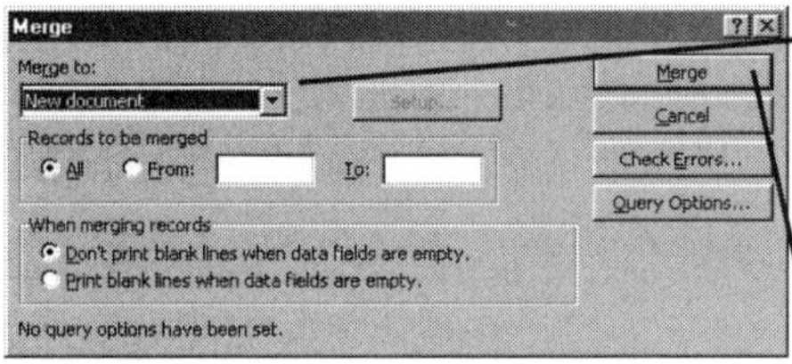

1. Click the Mail Merge toolbar's Merge button. Word displays the Merge dialog box.
2. Select an option from the Merge To drop-down list box to indicate whether Word should create a new document or simply send stuff to the printer, fax it, or e-mail it.
3. Click Merge, and then stand back. Word runs the mail merge and creates or prints the documents you described.

Margins

The page margins control how much white space appears around the edges of your page. By declaring a border of page space essentially "off limits," you control how much "printable" space remains.

Changing Page Margins

Choose the File menu's Page Setup command, and click the Margins tab to display a dialog box you'll use to specify page margins for printed documents.

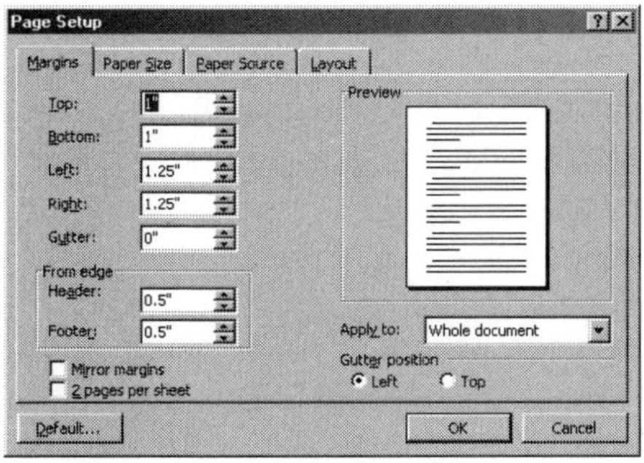

1 Enter an amount in the Top, Bottom, Left, and Right boxes to specify the margins in inches. If you want to specify a gutter, enter an amount in the Gutter box.

2 Enter an amount in the Header box to specify how many inches a header should be from the top of the page. Enter an amount in the Footer box to specify how many inches a footer should be from the bottom of the page.

3 Select the Mirror Margins check box if you will be printing on both sides of each page and want the margins of facing pages to mirror each other.

4 Select an option from the Apply To drop-down list box to specify whether the margin change should apply to the entire document, to the current section only (if applicable), or only from the location of the insertion point onward. If text is selected, the first (and default) option is Selected Text.

SEE ALSO Printing

Margin gutters

A gutter is simply an extra margin along the edge of a page that's bound. You add gutter margins so that the binding doesn't hide part of the printed document or make the visible page margins look unbalanced.

Master Document

A master document is a document that combines other documents, called subdocuments, into one document. I don't cover master documents in this Pocket Guide. For more information, see your Word user documentation.

Microsoft Excel SEE Excel

Microsoft on the Web

If your computer connects to the Internet through either a local area network or a modem, you can get Word help via the **World Wide Web.** To get this type of help, choose the Help menu's Office On The Web command.

SEE ALSO Web Page

Moving Pictures

You can easily move drawing objects and pictures with the mouse: simply select the object or picture. Word adds selection handles to the object or picture to show that you've selected it. Then drag it to wherever you want it.

The selection handles are the little squares appearing at the corners and along each edge.

Moving pictures between documents

You can also move a graphics object or a picture by choosing the Edit menu's Cut and Paste commands in the same way as when you move other types of data.

SEE ALSO Drawing

Moving Text

You can move text by using either the drag-and-drop method or the Edit menu's Cut and Paste commands. Refer to the **Drag-and-Drop** entry if you want to use the mouse and a few deft clicks to move text.

If you want to use the Edit menu's Cut and Paste commands, follow these steps:

1. Select the text you want to move.
2. Choose the Edit menu's Cut command.
3. Position the insertion point where you want to move whatever it is you're moving.
4. Choose the Edit menu's Paste command.

SEE ALSO Clipboard; Copying Text

My Documents

Windows supplies a folder, named My Documents, that it expects you'll use for storing many of the documents you create. Based on this assumption, Word File menu's Open Document and Save Document dialog boxes both provide a My Documents shortcut you can use to quickly open the My Documents folder.

Navigation Keys

Your keyboard navigation keys can be a quick and precise way to reposition the **insertion point.** Here are a few of them:

Key or key combination	Where it moves the insertion point
Direction keys	One character or one line in the direction of the arrow
Ctrl + ←	Previous word
Ctrl + →	Next word
Ctrl + ↑	Previous paragraph
Ctrl + ↓	Next paragraph
Home	Start of line
End	End of line
PgUp and PgDn	Previous screen or next screen
Ctrl + Home	First character in document
Ctrl + End	Last character in document

Nonbreaking Spaces

Word wraps your lines of text. When you get to the end of a line—if you're in the middle of typing a long word such as *Madagascar,* for example—Word moves the big word to the next line, where there's ample room. Word figures that it's fine with you if it breaks your lines of text between words, where there are spaces. Usually, Word is right.

You can, however, use something called a nonbreaking space if you don't want Word to break a line between two particular words. To do this, hold down the Ctrl and Shift keys while you press the Spacebar; or choose the Insert menu's Symbol command, click the Special Characters tab, and select Nonbreaking Space from the list box. Word places a space in the document—just as though you had pressed only the Spacebar—but Word won't break the line at this space. It'll use one of the other spaces in the line.

SEE ALSO Word Wrap

Nonprinting Characters

Most of what you type in a Word document gets printed. But if you think about it for a minute or so, you'll realize that not everything you enter gets printed. Consider, for example, the case of the Enter key. Word has no Enter character. When you press Enter, what you've really done is tell Word that a **paragraph** ends at the current **insertion point** location.

Although you may not see anything in the document that shows the end of a paragraph, Word places a special, nonprinting character in the document which basically indicates that the user wants the paragraph to end there. Word also places other characters in a document for keys you type but that Word doesn't print—tabs and spaces are the most common.

To see these nonprinting characters, choose the Tools menu's Options command, click the View tab, and then select the Formatting Marks check boxes. Or you can just click the Show/Hide ¶ toolbar button.

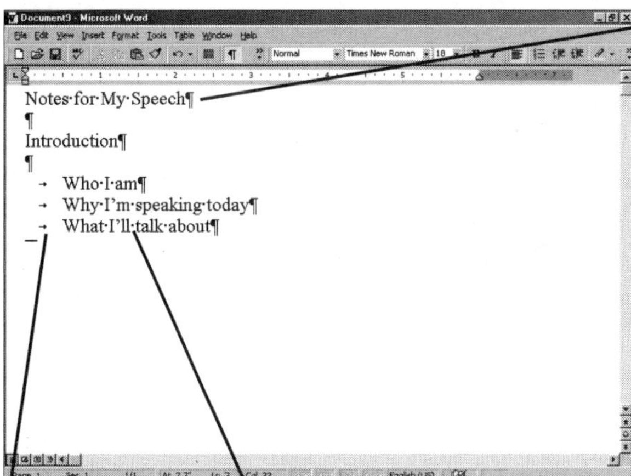

An end-of-paragraph character, which you enter by pressing Enter.

A tab character.

A space character.

Numbered Lists

You can create numbered lists of **paragraphs.** (Each paragraph is considered a list entry.)

Creating a Numbered List

To create a numbered list, select the **paragraphs** you want in the list. Then choose the Format menu's Bullets And Numbering command, and click the Numbered tab. Click one of the numbered list examples.

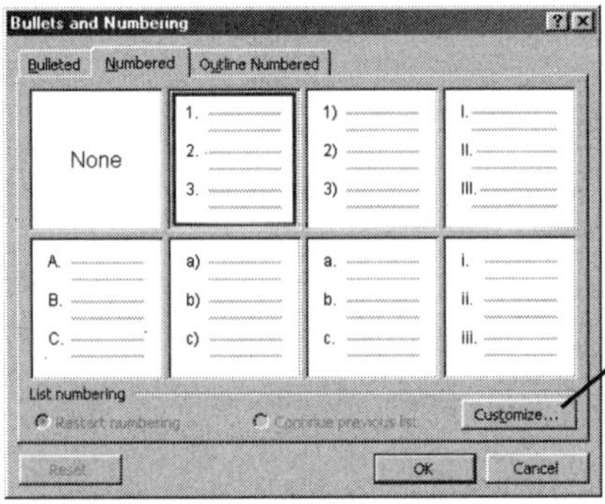

If you want, you can click Customize to specify numbering style, starting number, number position, and indentation.

Adding Numbered List Entries

To add an entry to a numbered list, place the insertion point at the end of an existing entry, press Enter, and then type the new list entry. Word automatically renumbers the items in a numbered list as you add and remove items.

Removing Numbered List Entries

To remove an entry from a numbered list, select it and press Delete.

SEE ALSO Bulleted Lists

Object

You can use objects to create what's called a compound document—a document file that combines two or more types of information. For example, you might want to create a compound document that includes a long report written in, for example, Microsoft Word. On page 27 of your report, however, you might want to include a worksheet or worksheet fragment created in Excel. On page 37 of your report, you might want to include a chart created in Excel. So your compound document consists of portions of information created in different programs—portions called objects—and pasted together in one big compound document.

Creating Compound Documents

To do all this pasting and combining, you can often use the program's Copy and Paste (or Paste Special) commands on the Edit menu. And if you're creating the compound document in Word, you can choose the Insert menu's Object command.

Distinguishing Between Linked Objects and Embedded Objects

A linked object—remember that it might be the Excel worksheet you've pasted into a word-processing document—gets updated whenever the source document changes. An embedded object doesn't. (You can, however, double-click an embedded object to open the application that created the embedded object to make your changes.)

Let me also make what may be an obvious point. If you embed, or copy, objects into a compound document, it gets bigger. When you simply link objects, the compound document doesn't really get bigger.

What you absolutely need to know about objects

Perhaps the most important tidbit for you to know about objects is that they're very easy to use. You don't have to do anything other than copy and paste the elements—the objects—you want to place in the compound document.

SEE ALSO **Embedding and Linking Existing Objects; Embedding New Objects**

Office Art

Microsoft Office 2000's better-than-ever new **drawing** applet, Office Art, comes with Word. Click the Drawing toolbar button to start Office Art and display the Drawing toolbar.

SEE ALSO Drawing

Office Assistant

Microsoft Word Help is now supplied by the Office Assistant, an animated character that pops up whenever you click the Help toolbar button or choose the Help menu's Microsoft Word Help command. When the Assistant appears, type a question and click Search. The Assistant will display the help topics that most closely relate to your question. Or click Tips, and the Assistant will display a series of tips that help you get the most from Word.

You can customize the Office Assistant to suit your preferences by using the Office Assistant dialog box.

Choosing an Assistant

To pick the particular Assistant you like, right-click the Assistant and choose the shortcut menu's Choose Assistant command. You can choose an Assistant from a gallery of available characters on the Gallery tab of the Office Assistant dialog box.

Setting Assistant Options

By clicking the shortcut menu's Options command, you display the Options tab of the Office Assistant dialog box, where you can set a variety of options relating to the Assistant's capabilities. You can also set options that control how tips are displayed.

Hiding the Assistant

Microsoft research shows that people either like or dislike the Office Assistant. If you find that you don't like it, you can tell Word not to display the Office Assistant. To do this, right-click the Office Assistant and then choose Hide Assistant from the shortcut menu.

SEE ALSO Help; Tips

Office Server Extensions

The newest version of Word works with Office Server Extensions. Office Server Extensions and a related feature called WebPost, available in each of the Microsoft Office 2000 programs, let you save Office documents to and retrieve Office documents from a web server. Note, however, that Office Server Extensions should be transparent to Word users. The Office Server Extensions aren't something Word users need to work with directly. Office Server Extensions run on the web server and typically are monitored and maintained by the network or web server administrator.

Opening Documents

To open a previously saved document, choose the File menu's Open command. Or click the Open toolbar button. Either way, Word displays the Open dialog box, shown below.

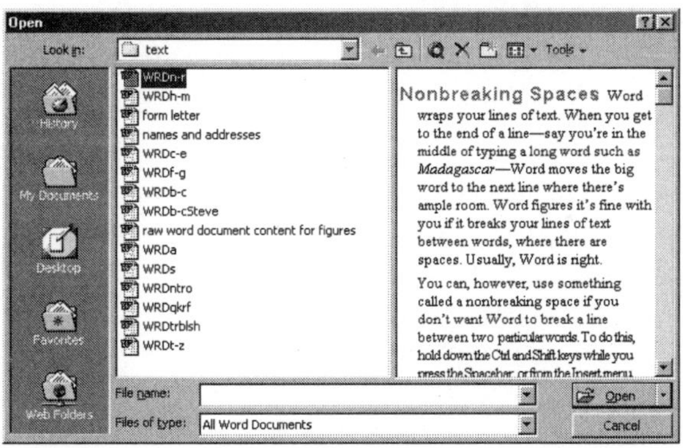

1 Click the **History, My Documents, Desktop, Favorites,** or **Web Folder** shortcut icon to specify where the document is located if you've previously saved, opened, or viewed the file; stored it in the My Documents folder; stored it on your desktop; added it to your Favorites folder; or retrieved it from a web folder. Or, alternatively, specify where the document file was saved in the Look In boxes.

2 If necessary, select a file type from the Files Of Type list box if you want to open a file with a format other than that of the usual Word document file. (You might do this if you want to import another word processor's document file.)

3 When you see the document file in the file list box, double-click it to open it. Or, alternatively, enter the document's name in the File Name text box, and click Open.

continues

Opening Documents *(continued)*

Protecting the original document

If you don't want to overwrite the original document file, click the down arrow at the right end of the Open button and then choose the drop-down menu's Open Read Only command. If you choose Open Read Only and later want to save the document, you'll need to use a new filename.

Numbered File menu commands

Word provides numbered File menu commands for opening the last four documents you opened. With a couple of quick clicks, you can open one of these documents.

SEE ALSO **File Properties; Saving Documents; Troubleshooting: You Can't Find a Document**

Opening New Documents

To create a new document, choose the File menu's New command or click the New Blank Document toolbar button.

If you choose the File menu's New command, Word displays the New dialog box. Select a document **template** that uses **formatting** close to the formatting you want for your new document. Word provides a number of different templates, including publication, letter and faxes, résumé, memo, report, and **web page** templates. To choose one of these templates, just click the appropriate tab and then click a template icon in the large box. If you don't know what formatting you want for your new document, click Blank Document on the General tab. Then click OK. You're done.

SEE ALSO **Opening Documents; Wizards**

Orphan

In printed documents, an orphan occurs when the first line of a **paragraph** prints on one page and the rest of the paragraph prints on the next page. Choose the Format menu's Paragraph command, and click the **Line And Page Breaks** tab. Select the Widow/Orphan Control check box to tell Word to eliminate orphans by always breaking paragraphs so that at least the first two lines of any given paragraph get printed on the same page.

SEE ALSO **Widow**

Outlining

Word makes it easy to create an outline, and it's easy to change an outline, too—condensing it, expanding it, and revising it, for example. To create an outline, first provide—as you would do if you were creating an outline with paper and pencil—headings for the parts of your document; for example, the chapter titles for a book. Then provide subheadings for each of the headings. If necessary, continue this process by providing sub-subheadings for each of the subheadings.

Creating an Outline

To create an outline, follow these steps:

1. Create a new **document** based on the Normal document **template** by choosing the File menu's New command and pressing Enter.
2. Choose the View menu's Outline command. Word displays the document in Outline view and adds the Outlining **toolbar** to the **program window.**
3. Enter the lines of text that describe each major and minor part within the document. (Each line of text should be entered as a **paragraph.**)
4. Indent the subparts within a part by selecting the parts you want to indent and then clicking the Demote toolbar button.

continues

Outlining *(continued)*

Using the Outlining Toolbar Buttons

The Outlining toolbar provides a series of buttons you'll find useful for creating and revising outlines. Note that because you end an outline level by pressing Enter, each outline level is actually a paragraph.

Tool	What it does
	Promotes the selected paragraph to the next higher outline level.
	Demotes the selected paragraph to the next lower outline level.
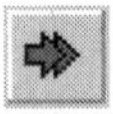	Demotes the selected paragraph to the lowest outline level, which is document body text.
	Moves the selected paragraph so that it's immediately above the preceding paragraph.
	Moves the selected paragraph so that it's immediately below the following paragraph.
	Displays the next lower outline level if it has previously been hidden.
	Hides the next lower outline level.
1	Displays all the heading 1 levels in the outline.
2	Displays all the heading 1 and 2 levels in the outline.
3	Displays all the heading 1–3 levels in the outline.
4	Displays all the heading 1–4 levels in the outline.
5	Displays all the heading 1–5 levels in the outline.
6	Displays all the heading 1–6 levels in the outline.
7	Displays all the heading 1–7 levels in the outline.
All	Displays all the heading levels in the outline.

Tool	What it does
	Displays only the first line of each paragraph of body text.
	Toggles the displayed (but not the printed) formatting of all text between formatted and unformatted.

Master documents

In addition to the Outlining toolbar buttons already described, Word also provides some tools on the Outlining toolbar for working with master documents. The master document toolbar buttons aren't described in the preceding table.

Beginning Your Writing

To begin your writing, choose the View menu's Normal or View Page Layout command. Word uses the parts, subparts, and sub-subparts you entered to create the outline as headings in the document. Then you simply type the paragraphs of text that follow the headings.

Tables of contents and outlines

One other advantage of the Word outlining feature is that when you use it you can generate a table of contents almost automatically. To do this, place the insertion point where you want the table of contents to be generated, choose the Insert menu's Index And Tables command, click the Table Of Contents tab, and then click OK.

Page Borders

With Word's new Page Borders feature, now you can add a fantastic array of plain or decorative borders to the margins of your pages. The Word collection of page art has plenty of choices for most any taste and occasion, and page borders are so easy to use that if you're an aesthete, it may be your favorite feature in the new Word. To add a border around your page, follow these steps:

1. Choose the Format menu's Borders And Shading command. Word displays the Borders And Shading dialog box.
2. Click the Page Border tab.

continues

Page Borders *(continued)*

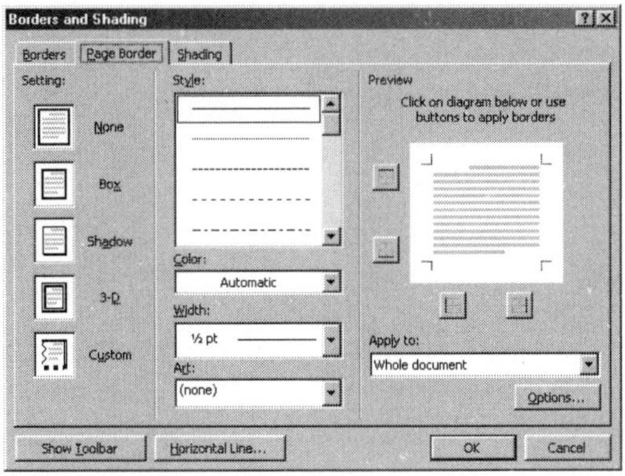

3 Click a Setting option to select the Box border, Shadow border, 3-D border, or Custom border. For a fancier border, select a design from the Art drop-down list box.

4 Select options from the Style, Color, and Width list boxes to specify a thickness for the border and a color (if you want something besides basic black).

5 Select an option from the Apply To drop-down list box to add borders to the whole document or part of the document.

6 Click Options to set the border's distance from the edge of the page or from the text.

7 Click OK.

SEE ALSO **Paragraph Borders; Picture Borders; Table Borders**

Page Breaks

Page breaks are the points where the document text breaks from one page to the next.

Automatic Page Breaks

Word automatically adds page breaks as you create your document. Automatic page breaks appear in the document as dotted lines.

Manual, or Hard, Page Breaks

You can add a manual, or hard, page break. To do so, position the **insertion point** at the spot where the page break should precede (usually the start of a line), choose the Insert menu's Break command, click Page Break, and then click OK. An even faster way to do this is to press Ctrl+Enter. Word identifies page breaks you've added this way by placing the words *Page Break* on the dotted page-break line.

Removing page breaks

You can remove hard page breaks. To do so, select the page break and then press Delete.

Page Numbers

You can number your document pages. To do this, follow these steps:

1 Choose the Insert menu's Page Numbers command.

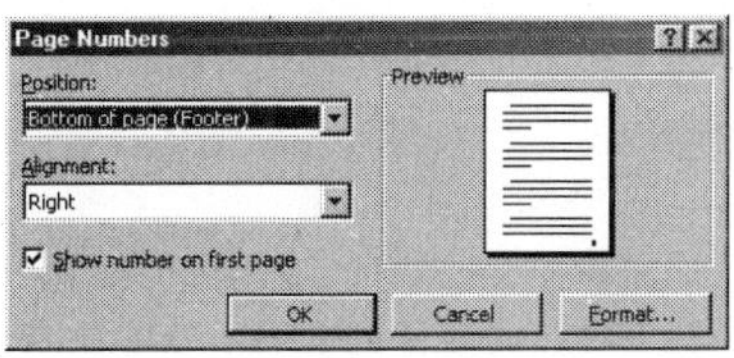

2 Select a position from the Position drop-down list box to place the page numbers.

3 Select an alignment option from the Alignment drop-down list box to specify how page numbers should be aligned.

4 Select the Show Number On First Page check box to indicate whether the first page should have a printed page number.

5 Click Format if you want text in your pagination or if you want to start with a page number other than 1.

Where page numbers go

Page numbers appear in either the header or the footer. In effect, when you insert page numbers, you add a header or a footer that shows the page number.

Page Orientation

The orientation of a page is either vertical (portrait) or horizontal (landscape). To select page orientation, choose the File menu's Page Setup command, click the Paper Size tab, and then click either Portrait or Landscape. If you're not sure which orientation you want, simply look at the Preview box. It shows how the printed page changes as you click option buttons under Orientation.

Page Tab

If a dialog box contains more options than will fit within its borders, the dialog box uses several pages, or tabs. Each page tab displays a related set of needed input information. You can move through these pages by clicking the tabs. To see an example of how this works, choose the File menu's Page Setup command and then click the Margins, Paper Size, Paper Source, and Layout tabs.

Pagination

Pagination refers to the process of breaking a document into page-size portions. You can let Word paginate your documents. Or you can do it yourself by using hard page breaks. If you do use hard page breaks and you add or delete text, you may have to adjust them by hand.

SEE ALSO Page Breaks

Paragraph and Line Spacing

Remember that every time you press Enter, you send a signal to Word that you've ended a paragraph. If you want to automatically add some space before or after these paragraphs, you can use the Format menu's Paragraph command.

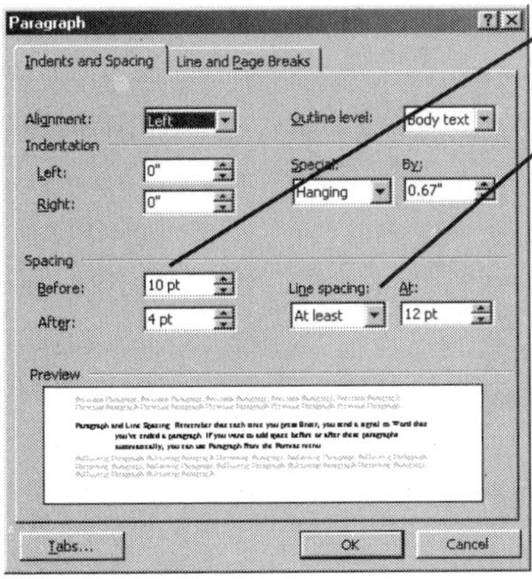

Use the Before and After boxes to specify the paragraph spacing in points.

Use the Line Spacing and At boxes to specify the line spacing.

Paragraph Borders

You can add border lines to paragraphs. To do so, follow these steps:

1 Select the paragraph.

2 Choose the Format menu's Borders And Shading command. Word displays the Borders And Shading dialog box.

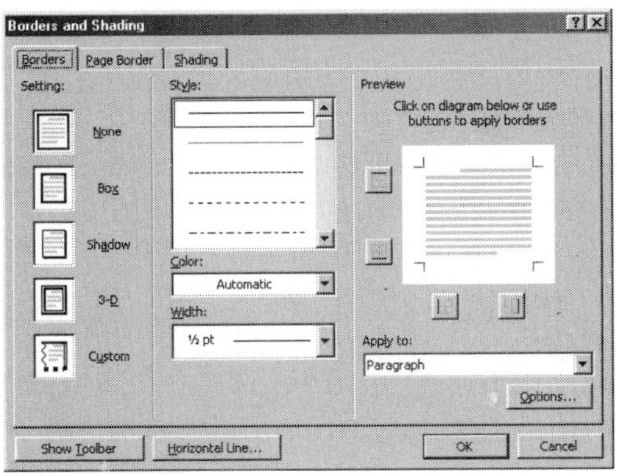

3 Click the Borders tab.

4 Click a Setting option to select the Box border, Shadow border, 3-D border, or Custom border. The Preview box shows the position and layout of your border choice.

continues

Paragraph Borders *(continued)*

5 Select options from the Style, Color, and Width boxes to specify a border line style, color (if you want something besides basic black), and thickness.

6 If you select the Custom border, use Preview to tell Word where to draw the border.

7 Click Options if you want to adjust how much white space should separate the border and the text. (One point equals 1/72 inch.)

8 Or click Show Toolbar to draw a border by using the Tables And Borders toolbar.

SEE ALSO **Page Borders; Picture Borders**

Paragraphs

In prose, a paragraph is a group of sentences. Ideally, a paragraph starts with a topic sentence and develops a single thought. High-school composition, so I hear, was a breeze if you could write solid, well-structured paragraphs.

In Word, a paragraph is simply a portion of text that ends wherever you press Enter. This means that a paragraph can have a single character, a sentence, or a group of sentences. All you have to do is press Enter.

All this may seem like much ado about nothing, but you should remember what paragraphs are—at least from the Word point of view. The reason is that much of the **formatting** you do in Word applies to paragraphs. You can, for example, format paragraphs by changing indents, line spacing, and alignment. You can also control the way **pagination** affects your paragraph.

SEE ALSO **Indentation and Alignment; Paragraph and Line Spacing; Widow**

Passwords

You can use passwords to limit access to a file and to limit changes to a document. To control access to a file, choose the File menu's Save As command. Click the Tools toolbar button, and choose the submenu's General Options command. Enter a password in the Password To Open or Password To Modify text boxes. To control and limit changes to a document's text, choose the Tools menu's Protect Document command.

SEE ALSO Protecting Documents; Save Options

Pathname

A pathname describes the location of a file on your computer or, if you're working on a local area network, on the network. Office programs such as Word let you use pathnames when you're **opening documents** and **saving documents**—you simply enter the pathname in the File Name box.

A pathname typically consists of three parts: the disk drive letter, the folder name, and the filename. If a file named letters.htm is stored in a folder named correspondence and this folder is located on the C disk drive, the pathname is

c:\correspondence\letters.htm

Note that the disk drive letter is separated from the folder name by a colon and a backslash and that the folder name is separated from the filename by a backslash. Note also that if a file is located in a subfolder, the subfolder or subfolders become part of the pathname, too. For example, if a file named letters.htm is stored in a subfolder named January, which is stored in a folder named correspondence, which is located on the C disk drive, the pathname is

c:\correspondence\january\letters.htm

Personal Menus and Toolbars

Word 2000 combines tools from the Standard toolbar and the Formatting toolbar to create a new Personal toolbar that is displayed beneath the menu bar. Word further customizes toolbars and menus by hiding the toolbar buttons and commands you don't use and displaying those you do use. Usually, this adaptability feature enhances your use of Word because toolbars and menus are less cluttered. If you don't find personalized menus and toolbars helpful, you can override the way Word modifies them by following the instructions located in the Troubleshooting section of this Pocket Guide.

SEE ALSO Troubleshooting: Your Menu Commands Disappear *and* Your Toolbar Buttons Appear or Disappear

Picture Borders

You can add border lines to pictures you've inserted in a document. Adding a picture border works just like adding a **paragraph border.**

Picture Bullets SEE Bulleted Lists

Points and Point Size

One point equals 1/72 inch. In Word, you specify font size and row height in points. You can also specify measurements in points for most dialog box entries by entering the number of points and then typing the letter *p*.

SEE ALSO Changing Fonts

Printing

To print the **document** displayed in the **document window,** choose the File menu's Print command or click the Print toolbar button. If you choose the File menu's Print command, Word displays the Print dialog box. To use the Print dialog box, follow these steps:

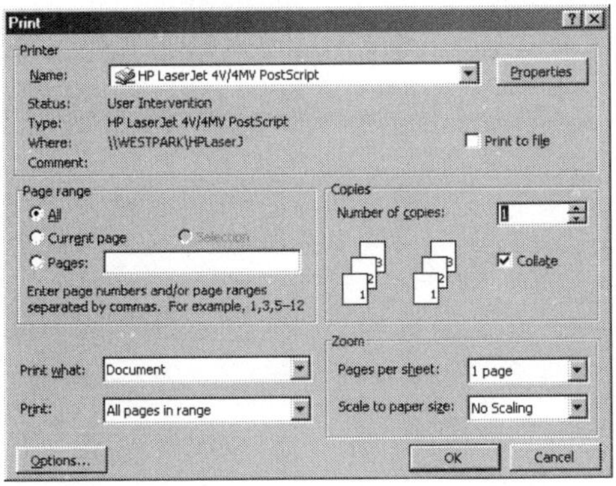

1. Select a printer from the Name drop-down list box to specify which printer Word should use if you have more than one printer on your system.
2. Select a Page Range option to specify what portion of a document should print. For example, if you want to print pages 2 through 8, click the Pages option button and enter *2-8* in the text box.
3. Enter an amount in the Copies box to specify how many copies of the document you want to print.
4. Select an option from the Print What drop-down list box to indicate whether you want to print the document—the usual choice—or something else related to the document, such as the file summary information or the styles list.
5. Select an option from the Pages Per Sheet drop-down list box to specify that you want to print more than one page of your document on a single piece of paper.

SEE ALSO Print Preview

Print Preview

You can use the File menu's Print Preview command or click the Print Preview toolbar button to see how a document's pages will look when they're printed. When you choose the command, Word displays a reduced image of the page in the middle of the **program window.** Use the PgUp and PgDn keys to move through the **document.** Click in the document to alternately enlarge or reduce the displayed page size. To turn off the Print Preview display, click Close.

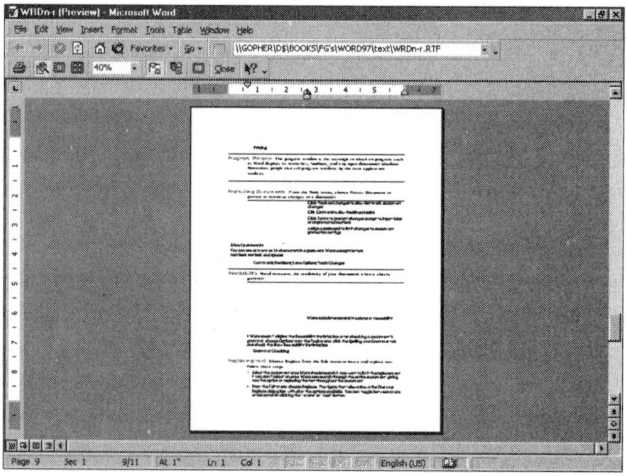

SEE ALSO Printing

Program Window

The program window is the rectangle in which a program such as Word displays its menu bar, **toolbars**, and any open **document windows.** Sometimes people also call program windows by the term **application windows.**

Protecting Documents

You can protect a document so that revisions aren't lost. To do this, choose the Tools menu's Protect Document command. When Word displays the Protect Document dialog box, click the Tracked Changes option button to allow document changes but mark them. If you want, you can also click the Comments option button to allow the addition of annotations and the Forms option button to prevent changes except to input fields or unprotected sections. Optionally, you can assign a password to limit changes to document protection settings.

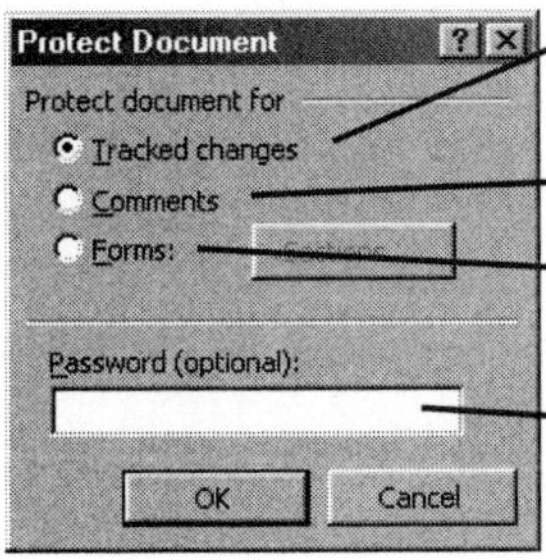

Click Tracked Changes to allow but mark document changes.

Click Comments to allow the addition of annotations.

Click Forms to prevent changes except to input fields or unprotected sections.

Assign a password to limit changes to document protection settings.

About passwords

You can use as many as 15 characters in a password. Word accepts letters, numbers, symbols, and spaces.

SEE ALSO Comments; Revisions; Save Options; Track Changes

Readability

Word measures the readability of your **document** when it checks grammar, providing several measures of readability, as shown in the Readability dialog box.

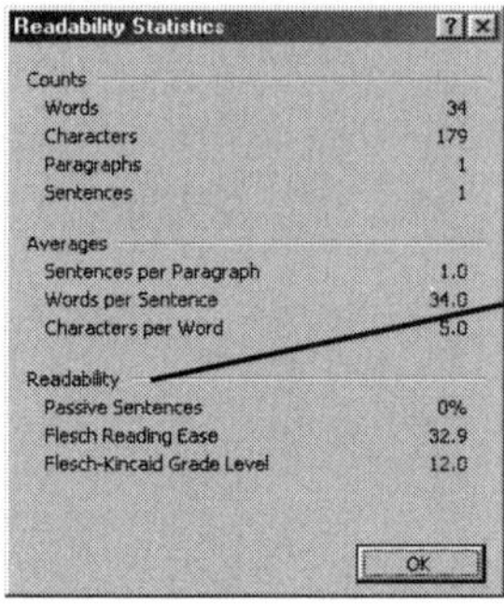

Word calculates several measures of readability.

If Word doesn't display the Readability Statistics box after checking a document's grammar, choose the Tools menu's Options command, click the Spelling And Grammar tab, and select the Show Readability Statistics check box.

SEE ALSO Grammar Checking

Replacing Text

You can replace document text by using the Edit menu's Replace command. To do so, follow these steps:

1. Select the document area Word should search if you want to limit the replacement. If you don't select an area, Word can search through the entire document, giving you the option of replacing the text throughout the document.
2. Choose the Edit menu's Replace command. The figure that follows shows the Find And Replace dialog box with the options available. You can toggle between more or less detail by clicking More or Less.

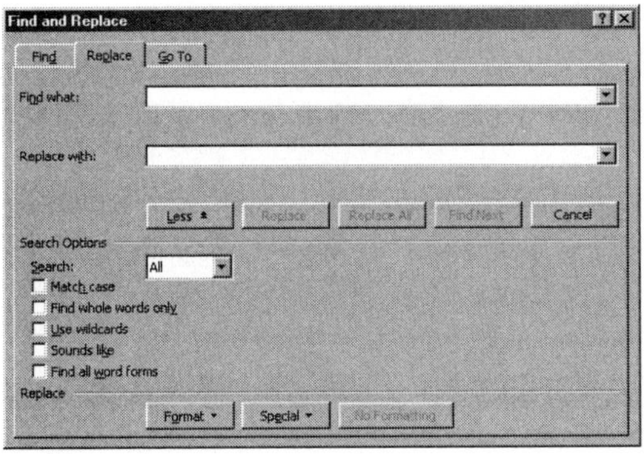

3 Enter text in the Find What box to specify what you want to replace.

4 Enter replacement text in the Replace With box.

5 Click More (if necessary), and select a direction from the Search drop-down list box to indicate whether Word should search downward (from the insertion point to the end of the document), upward (from the insertion point to the beginning of the document), or throughout the entire document.

6 Select the Match Case and Find Whole Words Only check boxes to indicate whether Word should consider case (lower vs. upper) in its search and look for only whole words rather than parts of words.

7 Click Find Next to start and restart the search.

8 Click Replace to substitute the replacement text.

9 Click Replace All to substitute the replacement text without your intervention.

SEE ALSO Finding Text

Replacing formatting

Usually, you'll use the Edit menu's Replace command to replace text. You can also use it to replace formatting. To do this, move the insertion point to the Find What box, click More if necessary, click Format, select a type of formatting from the list that Word displays, and then describe the formatting you're looking for. Then move the insertion point to the Replace With box, click Format, select a formatting option, and describe the replacement formatting.

Resizing Pictures

Use the mouse to resize pictures. To do this, select the picture. Word marks the picture with selection handles. (The selection handles show up as little squares.) To change the picture's size, drag the selection handles. (If you drag a side, top, or bottom handle, the proportions of the picture will also change. If you want to resize without messing up the proportions, grab a corner handle and drag diagonally.)

SEE ALSO Adding Document Pictures; Moving Pictures

Revisions

You can tell Word to keep track of the changes you make (or someone else makes) to a document.

Adding Revisions

The first time you want to make revision marks on a document, choose the Tools menu's Track Changes command and then choose the submenu's Highlight Changes command.

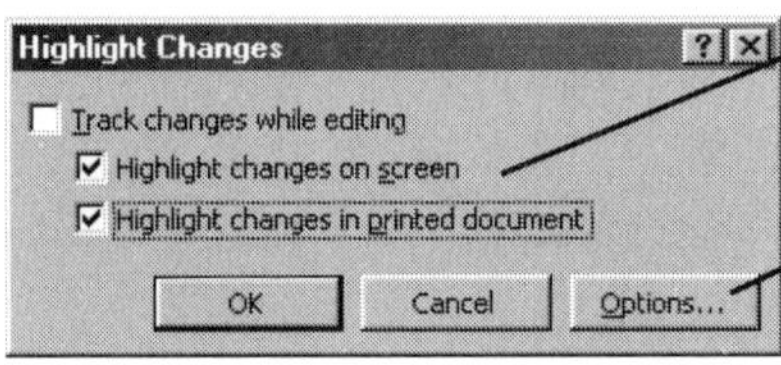

Select the check boxes to tell Word how and where it should show revisions.

Click Options to specify how Word marks revisions and differentiates multiple users' revisions.

After setting up your revision marks, you can go in and out of revision mode by double-clicking TRK on the status bar. Word draws vertical lines in the margins to flag lines with changed text, crosses out deleted text, and underlines new text.

To edit a document in a revision color, double-click TRK on the right side of the status bar. Double-click TRK again to leave Track Changes mode and revise in the default color.

Accepting or Rejecting Revisions

To review revisions, choose the Tools menu's Track Changes command and then choose the submenu's Accept Or Reject Changes command. Use the Find buttons to locate revised text. To accept a revision, click Accept. To reject a revision, click Reject. You can also use Accept All and Reject All to accept or reject all the revisions in a document. If you want to reverse a change, click Undo.

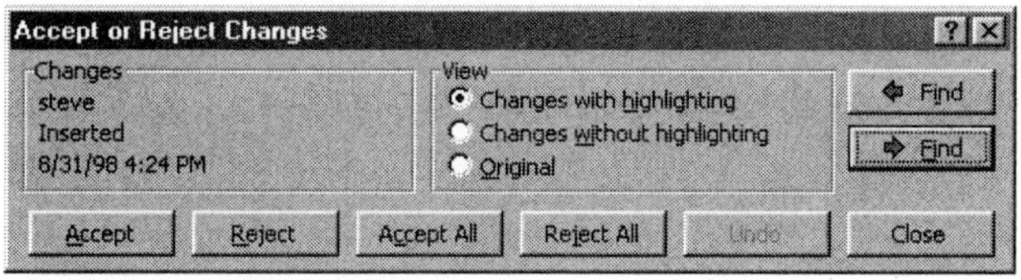

Right-Justify

You can right-justify text by telling Word that you want to use justified alignment. In this case, each line of text starts at the left margin and ends at the right margin. To do this, select the paragraphs you want to justify. Then click the Justify toolbar button.

SEE ALSO Indentation and Alignment

Ruler

The ruler appears below the **toolbar.** If you don't see the ruler (or if you see it but you want to get rid of it for now), choose the View menu's Ruler command.

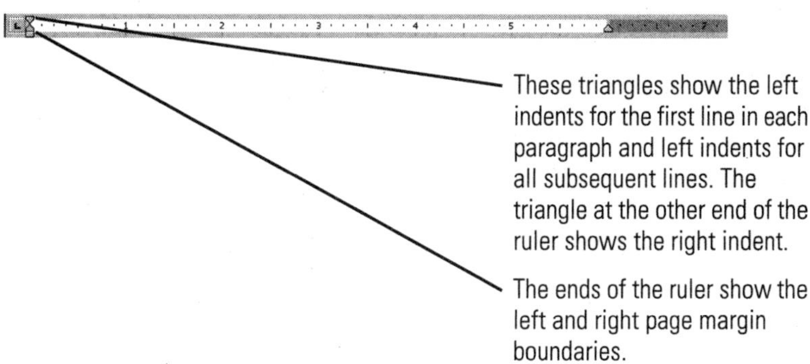

continues

Ruler *(continued)*

Changing indents and margins with the ruler

You can change indents and margins by using the ruler. To do so, drag the ruler's indent triangles and (if Word is in Page Layout view) margin boundaries.

SEE ALSO Indentation and Alignment; Margins

Save Options

The Save As dialog box provides a Tools button, which displays a menu of commands. You can use two of the commands, Web Options and General Options, to manage the way Word saves documents.

Specifying General Options

To specify whether a password should set up any other file-security measures, click Tools and then choose the General Options command. When Word displays the Save dialog box, follow these steps:

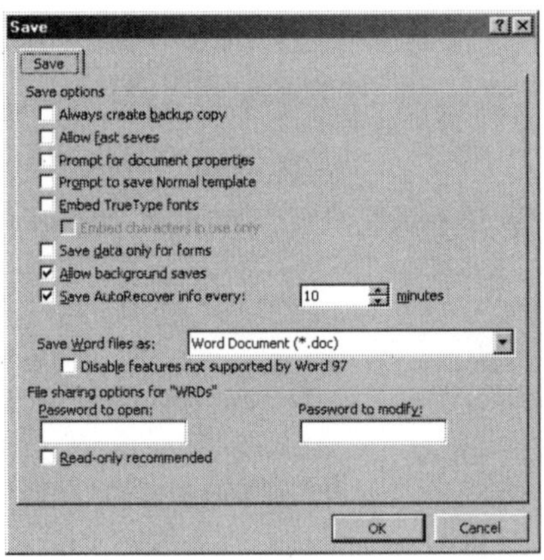

1. Select the Always Create Backup check box to create a backup copy of the existing, or old, document file whenever you save a new copy of the file.
2. You can limit viewing of the file by assigning a password in the Password To Open box. Word asks for the password when you choose the File menu's Open command.

3 Limit changes to when someone attempts to open the document file by assigning a password in the Password To Modify box. Word asks for the password when someone attempts to open the document file. Anyone who doesn't know the password can open the file only as Read Only. (Even with Password To Modify, someone can still save a copy of the document file with a new name.)
4 Select the Read-Only Recommended check box if you want Word to display a message which suggests that someone open the file with read-only privileges. By opening the document file as read-only, you can't save it later except by giving it a new name.

Specifying Web Options

To control how HTML versions of a Word document should be saved, choose the Tools menu's Web Options command. When Word displays the Web Options dialog box, use the General tab to specify the appearance and compatibility of the document, the Files tab to specify filename and location settings, the Pictures tab to specify graphics file format and target monitor information, and the Encoding tab to specify which alphabet should be used.

SEE ALSO File Properties; Saving Documents

Saving Documents

To save documents, choose the File menu's Save command or Save As command. Or you can also click the Save toolbar button.

Resaving a Document

Choose the File menu's Save command or click the Save toolbar button when you have already saved the document and want to save it using the same name and in the same location.

continues

Saving Documents *(continued)*

Saving a Document for the First Time

Choose the File menu's Save As command or click the Save toolbar button when you have created a new document and haven't yet saved it.

1 Specify where the workbook file should be placed by using either the shortcut icons—History, My Documents, Desktop, Favorites, or Web Folders—or the Save In box.

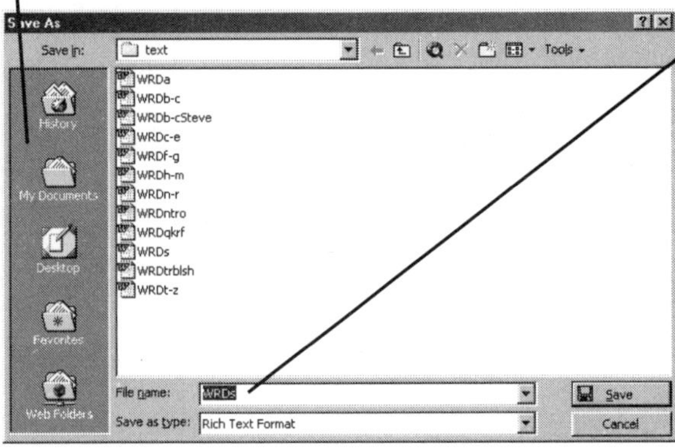

2 Name the document file, but don't enter the file extension. Word adds the file extension for you because it uses the extension to identify the file type.

3 Enter a filename in the Save As Type drop-down list box to save the file in a format other than the usual Word document file format. (Do this, for example, to use the document file with another word processor program.)

Renaming documents

Choose the File menu's Save As command when you want to save a copy of the document with a new name or in a new location.

SEE ALSO **Filenames; File Properties; Opening Documents; Save Options**

Saving Web Pages

You can save documents or document selections as **web pages,** even to the point of publishing a Word document to a web server so that other people can use the document. To save a Word document or document selection as a web page, choose the File menu's Save As Web Page command and then follow these steps:

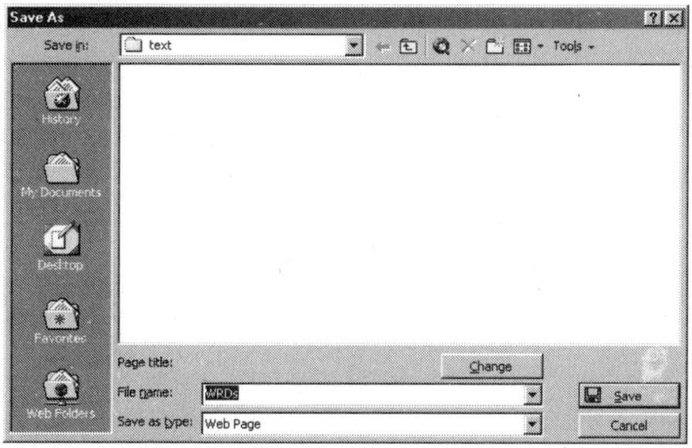

1. Specify where the document file should be placed by using either the shortcut icons—**History, My Documents, Desktop, Favorites,** or **Web Folders**—or the Save In box.
2. Click Change to display a dialog box you can use to give the web page a name.
3. Enter a name for the new web page in the File Name drop-down list box.
4. Verify that the Save As type drop-down list box indicates that you're saving a web page.
5. Name the document file, but don't enter the file extension. Word adds the file extension for you because it uses the extension to identify the file type.
6. Click Save to save the Word document by using the HTML file format.

SEE ALSO **Save Options; Saving Documents**

Scrolling

Scrolling simply refers to paging through a **document.** You can move the vertical scroll bars with your mouse. You can also press the PgUp and PgDn keys—or one of the other **navigation keys** or key combinations. Or you can choose the Edit menu's **Go To** command.

Sections

You can break Word documents into parts, or sections. To do this, choose the Insert menu's Break command. Then select the option for the type of section break you want.

Sections can seem kind of funny. I think that section breaks are most useful for headers and footers. If you set up a header or a footer for a file, it will apply to every page unless it has a section break, in which case you can change the header or footer. Some people use sections to lay out pages differently—for example, by using different margins.

Selecting

When you want to move, copy, delete, or format some element of a Word document, you need to select it first. The easiest way to do this is by clicking and sometimes dragging the mouse.

Selecting Words

Select words by double-clicking them with the mouse.

Selecting Line Fragments

Select blocks of text—including single characters—by clicking in front of the first character and then dragging the mouse to just after the last character. Word flip-flops the colors of selected text—black becomes white, and white becomes black—to highlight your selection.

Selecting Sentences

Select a sentence by holding down Ctrl while you click the sentence.

Selecting a Single Line of Text

Select a line of text by clicking in the selection bar (the area directly to the left of text) adjacent to the line.

Selecting Multiple Lines of Text

Select multiple lines of text by clicking the selection bar and dragging the mouse.

Selecting Paragraphs

You can select an entire paragraph by double-clicking the selection bar next to the paragraph. Or you can triple-click anywhere in the paragraph.

Selecting Objects and Pictures

Select objects and pictures by clicking them. Objects and pictures show selection handles (little squares on their corners and sides).

When in doubt about how to select

If you don't know how to select something, try clicking it. Or try dragging the mouse over it.

Shortcut Menus

Word knows which commands make sense in which situations. It also knows which commands that you, as a Word user, are most likely to use. If you want Word to, it will display a menu of these commands—called the shortcut menu. All you need to do is click the right mouse button. Remember that you use the left mouse button for selecting menus, commands, dialog box elements, and other assorted and sundry items.

Sorting

You can sort **paragraphs** and **table** rows by choosing the Table menu's Sort command.

Sorting Paragraphs

To sort **paragraphs**—remember that a paragraph in Word is simply a portion of text that you end by—follow these steps:

1 Select the paragraphs you want to sort.

2 Choose the Table menu's Sort command.

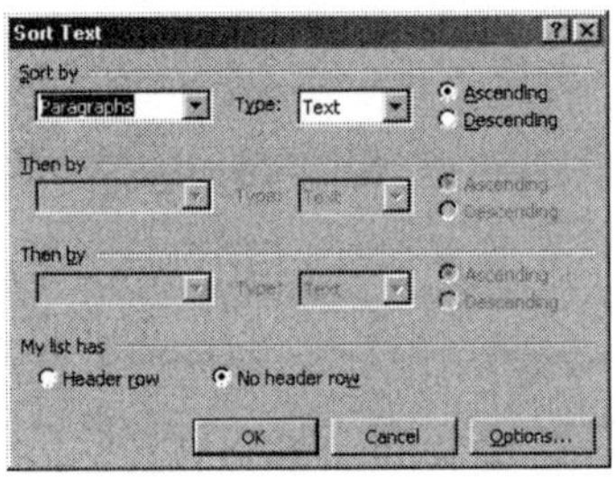

3 Select an entry from the Type drop-down list box to tell Word how paragraphs should be sorted: Choose the Text entry if you want to sort alphabetically by the letters that start the paragraphs. You can also sort the paragraphs by using a date or a number if these are the pieces of data that start the paragraphs.

4 Tell Word whether paragraphs should be organized in A to Z (ascending) or Z to A (descending) order.

Sorting Table Rows

Sorting table rows can get a bit complicated. You need to follow these steps:

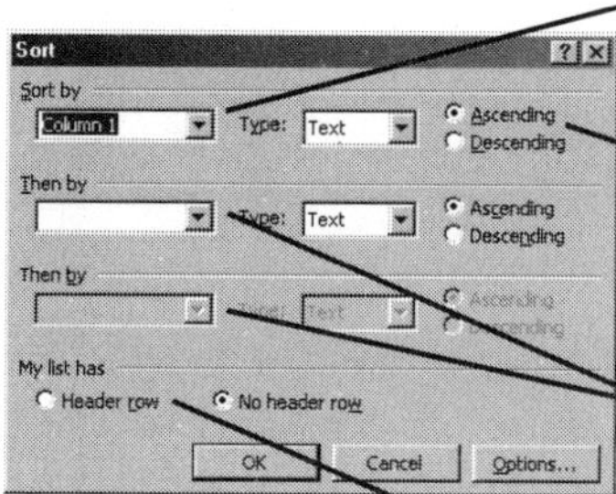

1. Select the table by placing the insertion point anywhere in the table and choosing the Table menu's Select command.
2. Choose the Table menu's Sort command.
3. Select an entry from the Sort By drop-down list box to name the column you use for alphabetizing or ordering.
4. Click an option button to the right of Sort By to indicate whether you want alphabetical list entries arranged in ascending (A to Z) or descending (Z to A) order.
5. Optionally, select entries from the Then By drop-down list boxes and click option buttons to add second and third items that Word will sort by.
6. Click an option button under My List Has to indicate whether the first selected row is a header that shouldn't be sorted.

Spelling SEE Automatic Spell Checking

Splitting Documents

If a document gets too large to work with comfortably, you can split it into two or more smaller documents. Before you do this, however, save the big document—just to be safe. Then follow the steps on the next page.

continues

Splitting Documents *(continued)*

1. Select a portion of the existing document that you want to move to a new document.
2. Click the Cut toolbar button to move the selected text to the Clipboard.
3. Open a new document—for example, by clicking the New toolbar button.
4. Click the Paste toolbar button so that the Clipboard contents are pasted into the new document.
5. Save the new document. (It now contains only what you cut and pasted from the original document.)
6. Save the original document. (It now contains only what remains after you cut and pasted a portion or portions of it into the new document.)

Using a master document

Word has another way to make documents more manageable. You can create a master document that uses subdocuments as its sections. If you're a casual user, however, you will not want to get this sophisticated. Still, be aware that the feature exists. You can find information about master documents in your Word user documentation.

SEE ALSO Clipboard; Opening New Documents; Saving Documents

Starting Word

You start Word the same way you start any Windows program.

Starting Word Manually

To start Word manually, follow these steps:

1. Click the Start button, and then choose Programs.
2. Choose Microsoft Office, and then choose Microsoft Word.

Starting Word Automatically

To have Word start every time you start Windows, follow these steps:

1. Click the Start button, and then choose Settings.
2. Choose the submenu's Taskbar command.
3. Click the Start Menu Programs tab in the Taskbar Properties dialog box.
4. Click Add, and then click Browse.
5. Find the Microsoft Word program icon in the large box under the Look In box, and then double-click the icon.
6. Click Next to close the dialog box, and then click the StartUp folder icon in the large box. Click Next.
7. Type *Word* (so that "Word" appears on the StartUp menu), and then click Finish.

Styles

Styles combine **font, paragraph, tab, border, frame,** language, and **numbered list** formats. You use styles so that you can simultaneously apply a combination of **formatting** changes to a document selection and so that you can easily change formatting throughout a **document.** One other tidbit you may find helpful to know about is that document **templates** are, for the most part, collections of styles.

SEE ALSO Applying Styles; Changing Styles; Creating Styles

Switching Tasks

To multitask, or run multiple programs at the same time, just open them. Click a program button on the Taskbar to switch to that application. Windows makes switching from one program window to another very easy. You can cycle through open applications by pressing Alt+Tab.

Symbols

You can use symbols in a document even if you don't see character keys on your keyboard for the symbols.

Adding Symbols

To add a symbol to a document, follow these steps:

1. Move the **insertion point** to the place where you want the symbol.
2. Choose the Insert menu's Symbol command.

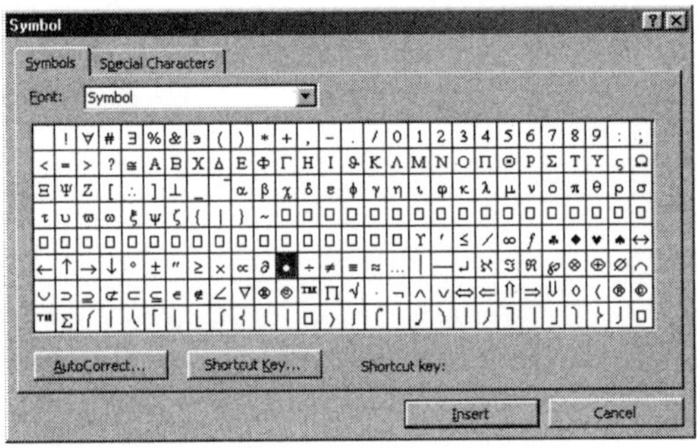

3. Click the Symbols tab if you want to use a symbol from one of the font character sets—such as one of the TrueType font sets.
4. Select a font from the Font drop-down list box. After you specify the font set, Word displays a grid of the characters. Word magnifies the selected character.
5. Select the character by clicking the mouse.
6. Click Insert to add the symbol to your document.
7. Repeat steps 5 and 6 to insert additional symbols.
8. Click Close to close the dialog box.

Deleting Symbols

Symbols are characters. To delete a symbol, select it and press Delete. Or press Backspace to delete the symbol.

Typesetting Characters

Click the Special Characters tab to display a list of typesetting characters, such as the en dash, the em dash, and the copyright symbol. Word displays a short list box in which you can select one of these characters.

Table Alignment

To change the way a table aligns against a page's margins, select the table and choose the Table menu's Table Properties command, click the Table tab, and then click Alignment buttons to specify how the table should align.

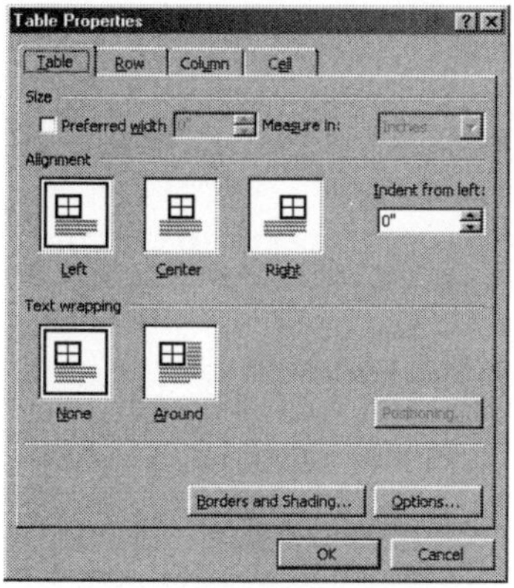

SEE ALSO Creating Tables

Table AutoFormats

You can have Word format the selected table. To do this, follow these steps:

1 Select the table.

2 Choose the Table menu's Table AutoFormat command.

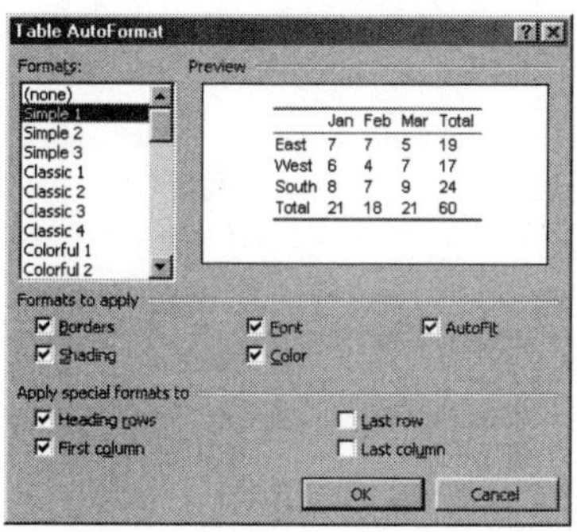

3 Select a format from the Formats list box.

continues

Table AutoFormats *(continued)*

4 Select or clear the check boxes under Formats To Apply to add or remove elements of the automatic formatting.

5 Select or clear the check boxes under Apply Special Formats To to remove formatting from specified columns and rows.

6 If the Preview box shows the formatting you want, click OK.

SEE ALSO Creating Tables

Table Borders

You can add border lines around tables and to the column and row edges in tables. To do so, follow these steps:

1 Select the table or whatever cells you want to format.

2 Choose the Format menu's Borders And Shading command.

3 Click the Borders tab.

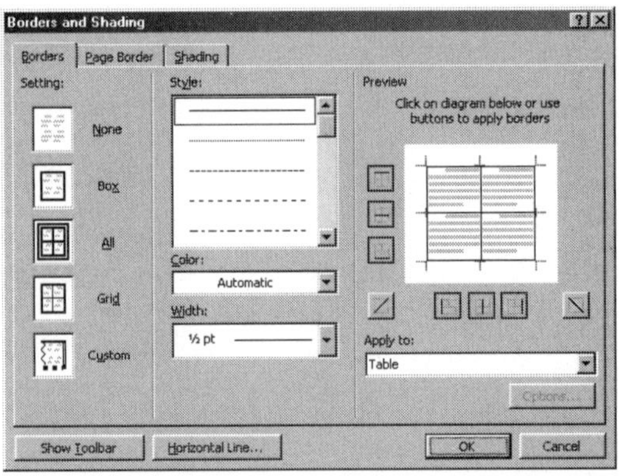

4 Click an option under Setting to choose a border option: Box, All, Grid, or Custom. Box draws a border around the table edge. All draws whatever border style you select around the table edge and between the columns and rows. Grid draws the selected border style around the table edge and a thinner line between the columns and rows. Custom lets you create a border using the options you click in the Preview box. The Preview box shows the position and layout of your border choice.

5 Select options from the Style, Color, and Width drop-down list boxes to specify a border line style, color, and thickness.

SEE ALSO Creating Tables

Table Columns

You can change the width of table columns easily and quickly. Simply select a column (for example, by clicking it and choosing the Table menu's Select command and then choosing the submenu's Column command), and then drag the column's right edge to change its width.

If you don't like to use the mouse or if you need to use exact measurements, you can select the column and then choose the Table menu's Table Properties command, click the Cell tab, and use the Preferred Width box to set the column width.

Merging and splitting table columns

You can merge the selected cells, including the selected columns, by choosing the Table menu's Merge Cells command. You can split the selected cells, including the selected columns, by choosing the Table menu's Split Cells command.

SEE ALSO **Creating Tables; Table Rows; Tables**

Table Headings

If a table gets broken across pages, you can tell Word to repeat the table's headings on the second and subsequent pages. To do this, select the row or rows that show the table headings and then choose the Table menu's Headings Row Repeat command. This command is a toggle switch—it turns the table headings feature on and off. To later remove the table headings, choose the command again.

SEE ALSO **Creating Tables**

Table Rows

You can change the height of table rows. To do this, follow these steps:

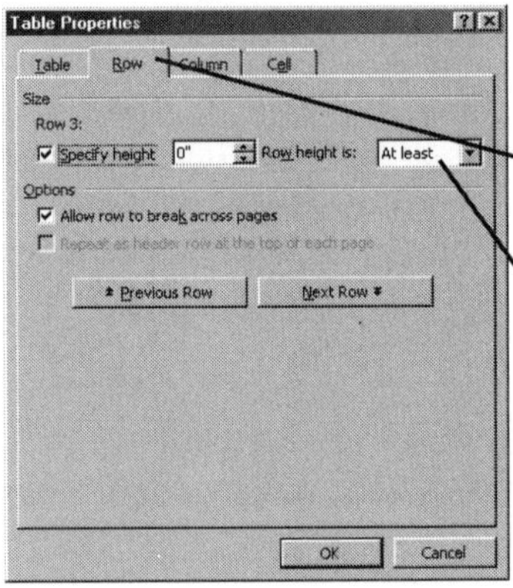

1. Select the row.
2. Choose the Table menu's Table Properties command.
3. Click the Row tab.
4. Enter the row height in the Specify Height box.
5. Select the At Least entry from the Row Height Is drop-down list box.

Merging and splitting table rows

You can merge the selected cells, including the selected rows, by choosing the Table menu's Merge Cells command. You can split the selected cells, including the selected rows, by choosing the Table menu's Split Cells command.

SEE ALSO Creating Tables; Table Columns; Tables

Tables

Tables use columns and rows to arrange information and have been around for years. Henry David Thoreau, for example, in his seminal work *Walden,* summarized the construction costs of his cabin with a table.

SEE ALSO Creating Tables; Formulas

Tables of Contents

A table of contents lists the parts that make up a document and gives the page numbers on which the parts start. In a novel, for example, the table of contents lists the chapters and gives the page numbers on which the chapters start.

Creating a Table of Contents Based on Outlines

If you use the Word **outlining** feature, you can create a table of contents by choosing the Insert menu's Index And Tables command, clicking the Table Of Contents tab (so that Word displays the Table Of Contents options), and then clicking OK. Clicking OK accepts the Word suggestions for table of contents organization and layout. Be sure to place the **insertion point** where you want the table of contents placed before telling Word to generate it.

Customizing a Table of Contents

You can also make changes to the organization Word suggests by using the Table Of Contents tab in the Index And Tables dialog box.

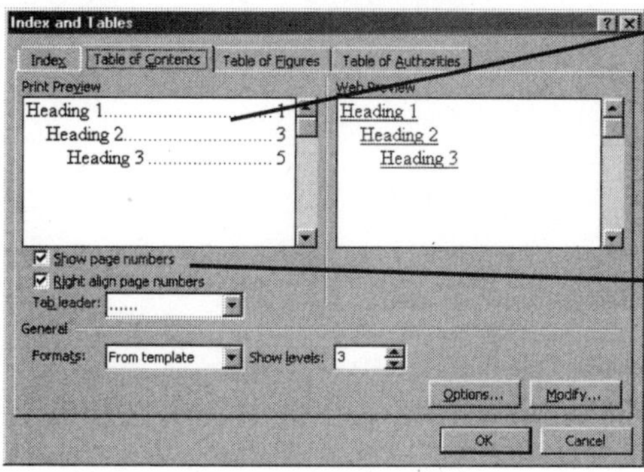

Select a table of contents style from the Formats drop-down list box, and look at the Preview boxes to see how your table of contents will look.

Select the Show Page Numbers and Right Align Page Numbers check boxes to tell Word whether and where you want page numbers.

continues

Tables of Contents *(continued)*

Creating a Table of Contents If You Didn't Outline

If you didn't use the Word outlining feature, you can still easily build a table of contents as long as you used heading **styles** for the document parts you want listed in your table. To do this, place the **insertion point** where you want the table of contents, choose the Insert menu's Index And Tables command (so that Word displays the Index And Tables dialog box), click the Table Of Contents tab, and then click Options (so that Word displays the Table Of Contents Options dialog box).

Select the Styles check box to tell Word that you want to build a table of contents using document styles.

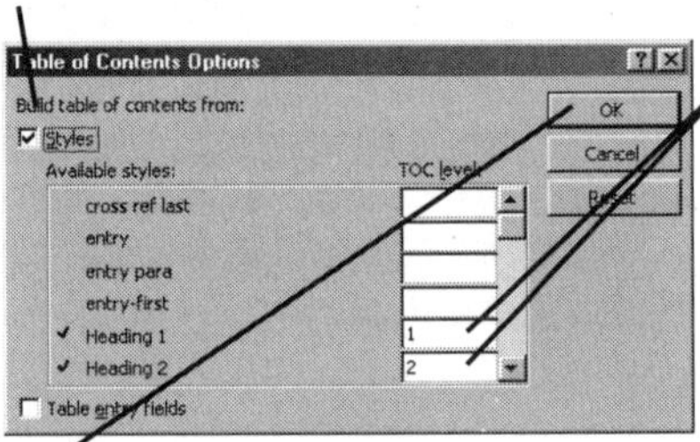

Indicate which styles should be listed in the table of contents by typing the number 1 in the highest-level style, the number 2 in the next-highest-level style, and so on.

Click OK to close the dialog box, and click OK again to build the table of contents.

Tabs

In the old days, you used the Tab key to move your typewriter carriage to the next tab stop. Typically, you did this for two reasons: to indent text—such as the first line of paragraphs—and to create **tables.** In Word, however, paragraph indenting is a **formatting** choice. (It saves you from having to press Tab.) You create tables by using the Table menu commands. Therefore, for most Word users, tabs are obsolete. You can indent in better and easier ways and create tables in easier and better ways.

SEE ALSO Indentation and Alignment

Templates

A template is a collection of **formatting** styles; **AutoText** entries; **macros** (if you or the template author have created any); and menu, shortcut, and toolbar changes (if you or the template author have made any).

When you start Word, it uses a template named Normal.dot to create a blank document. But by choosing the File menu's New command to create a new document, you can create a template based on some other tailored set of formatting styles. Word, for example, has templates for fax cover sheets, letters, press releases, reports, memos, and résumés.

SEE ALSO **Formulas; Styles**

Text Boxes

In Microsoft Word 97 and Word 2000, text boxes replace the **frames** used by previous versions of Word. Text boxes are drawing objects you create and modify with the **Drawing** toolbar. (Display the Drawing toolbar by clicking the Drawing toolbar button.) With this toolbar, you can use **Office Art** effects like 3-D, rotation, textured backgrounds, and fill color in your text boxes.

Themes

A theme is, essentially, a collection of styles and background colors and images you use to format electronic documents, such as **web pages.** To use a theme in a document—usually you'll want to do this before you add any text—choose the Format menu's Themes command. When Word displays the Theme dialog box, select the theme you want from the Choose A Theme list box.

Thesaurus

Use the Word Thesaurus to find synonyms for the selected word. To use the Thesaurus, select the word for which you want to find a synonym. Then choose the Tools menu's Language command and the submenu's Thesaurus command.

Use the Meanings list box to select the word description for which you want to find a synonym.

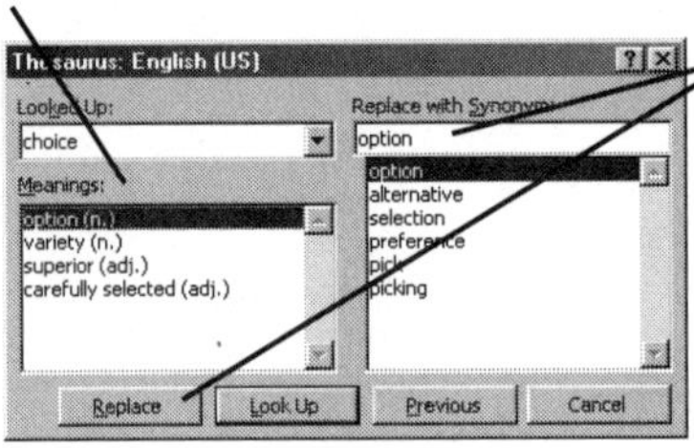

Use the Replace With Synonym list box to select the synonym you want to use in place of the word in the Looked Up box, and click Replace.

Times

You can enter a **field** for the current system time at the **insertion point** by pressing Alt+Shift+T. You can also choose the Insert menu's Date And Time command, but you need to select the Update Automatically check box to make the date a field. Either way, Word enters the time in HH:MM am/pm format. If it's 4 o'clock in the afternoon, for example, Word enters 4:00 PM.

SEE ALSO Dates

Tips

Word's **Office Assistant** will present you with a helpful nugget of knowledge about how to use Word, called a tip. To turn on the display of the Office Assistant's tips, click the Office Assistant and then click Options. When Word displays the Office Assistant dialog box, click the Options tab and then select the Show Tips check boxes. Note that to close a tip, you click its Close button.

Toolbars

Toolbars are those rows of buttons and boxes that appear at the top of your **program window,** just below the menu bar. Past versions of Word displayed two toolbars: the Standard toolbar and the Formatting toolbar. The current version of Word displays a single, Personal toolbar in place of the Standard and Formatting toolbars. Note that Word also provides several other toolbars. You can add and remove toolbars by pointing to any toolbar, clicking the right mouse button (rather than the usual left button), and then—when Word displays a list of the available toolbars—selecting the one you want. You can also use the View menu's Toolbars command to accomplish the same thing.

Toolbar button names

If you place the mouse pointer over a toolbar button, Word displays the button name in a tiny box, called a ScreenTip.

SEE ALSO Personal Menus and Toolbars

Track Changes

This submenu on Word's Tools menu supplies commands that let you make and compare **revisions** to documents. It's especially useful when more than one author is working on a document.

TrueType

TrueType scalable font technology was introduced by Apple Computer, Inc., in 1991 and by Microsoft Corporation in 1992. If you're working with Word, using TrueType fonts in your documents delivers two benefits. First, Word typically comes with several interesting and attractive TrueType fonts. Second, because of the way a scalable font is created, Word can easily change the point size in a way that results in legible fonts. Word identifies TrueType fonts with the prefix in the various Font list boxes.

SEE ALSO Changing Fonts; Fonts

Underline Characters

You can underline characters by selecting them and then either pressing Ctrl+U or clicking the Underline toolbar button. You can also choose the Format menu's Font command.

SEE ALSO Changing Fonts

Undo

You can undo your changes to a document one change at a time or in groups. To reverse document changes one change at a time, choose the Edit menu's Undo command. Or click the Undo toolbar button.

You can also undo selected changes or a series of changes by opening the Undo drop-down list box—click the down arrow to the right of the Undo toolbar button—and then selecting the last action you want to undo. Word undoes all the actions up to the action you selected.

Unicode

Unicode refers to an encoding standard that lets computers work with practically any characters used on a computer. Unicode therefore works with most of the languages in the world. It also works with just about any mathematical or technical symbols you will see. Microsoft Office programs, including Word, support the Unicode standard.

URL

The URL, short for Uniform Resource Locator, which specifies how you find an Internet resource, such as a World Wide Web page. A URL has four parts: the service, or protocol; the server name; the path; and the document, or file, name. To browse the Web or edit web documents, all you really need to care about is that URL is another term for an address on the Web.

Here's a sample of what a URL looks like:

http://us.imdb.com/search.html

This is the URL for the search page on the Internet Movie Database, a cool site with information about movies and filmographies of actors and directors.

Versions

With Word's Versioning feature, you can keep all versions of a particular document on file for easy reference, including versions saved by different users. To manage multiple versions of a document over time, open the document and then choose the File menu's Versions command. The Versions dialog box displays all existing versions of the document that have been recorded by using the Versions feature. The dialog box lists the date, time, and user, plus any comments the user may have made. To save a version for future tracking, click Save Now and then add any comments in the Save Version window that appears. To read a long comment, click View Comments. The Open and Delete boxes open or delete selected versions.

Virus

A virus is a malicious program that runs unknown to you and destroys or corrupts your data or files. Most computer viruses are "carried" by executable files that have been tampered with (an executable file is a file that runs an application). To protect against these files, you may want to get a frequently updated antivirus program like McAfee VirusScan. (You can download a demo for free from *http://www.mcafee.com* or buy the retail version at a computer store; either way, you should get an updated version every few months.) A new kind of virus has recently appeared. Usually known as the macro virus, this annoying form of virus can be contained in Word documents, or for that matter, in any documents containing executable commands. To prevent these, Word gives you the choice to disable any macros in a document before opening the document.

Visual Basic

Visual Basic is Word's built-in programming language. Visual Basic is very useful, but it's really a development tool for people with programming experience. For this reason, most users won't have occasion to work with it. Note, however, that most people can create and use powerful **macros** as a way to automate Word tasks.

Web Browser

A web browser is a program that lets you look at World Wide Web documents. Netscape Navigator and NCSA Mosaic are browsers, as is Microsoft Internet Explorer, which comes with Microsoft Office 2000. Most browsers let you browse, or view, both the graphics and text components of a **web page,** but some browsers let you look just at the text. (You might want to view only text if, for example, your connection to the Internet is slow—say, less than 28.8Kbps—or if you're interested in only the text portions of the documents you are viewing.)

Web Folder

The Web Folder shortcut icon, which appears in the Open Document, Save Document, and Save As Web Page dialog boxes, lists web server locations you can use for storing and retrieving Word documents.

SEE ALSO Opening Documents; Saving Documents; Saving Web Pages

---

Web Page

Web page is another name for a document on the **World Wide Web,** the most popular part of the Internet. Web pages often combine text, graphics, and other elements, including sound and movie or video clips. Web pages also usually include **hyperlinks,** or jumps, to other web pages.

SEE ALSO HTML

Web Page Preview

You can preview how a Word document will look as a web page by using your default **web browser.** To do so, choose the File menu's Web Page Preview command.

SEE ALSO Saving Web Pages

Widow

In printed **documents,** a widow occurs when the last line of a **paragraph** is printed on the next page. By choosing the Format menu's Paragraph command and clicking the **Line And Page Breaks** tab options, you can tell Word to eliminate widows by always breaking a paragraph so that at least two lines of it get printed on the next page.

SEE ALSO Orphan

Window Buttons

Arranged around the outside edge of the **application window** and **document windows** are buttons and icons. You can use them to display the **Control menu,** to close windows, and to minimize and change the window size, as listed in the following table:

Button or icon	Description
	Displays the Microsoft Word program's Control menu.
	Displays the document window's Control menu.
	Minimizes a window by turning it into a button.
	Restores a window to its previous size.
	Maximizes a window. Maximized program windows fill the screen. Maximized document windows fill the program window.
	Closes the window. By the way, closing a program window closes the program.

continues

Window Buttons *(continued)*

A quick exit

You can close a document window by clicking its Close button (the one with an X in it). You can close a program in exactly the same way.

Window Panes

You can split a **document window** into panes and then use the panes to view different portions of the document simultaneously. You might do this to view a document's **table of contents** (from page 1) in one pane and something from the fifth **section** of the document (for example, from page 21) in another pane.

Creating Window Panes

To split a window into panes, follow these steps:

1. Choose the Window menu's Split command to split the **active document** window into two panes. To show the split window, Word draws a thick, transparent, horizontal line through the middle of the document window.
2. Move the mouse pointer or press the Up and Down arrow keys to move this line to where you want the window to be split.
3. Click the mouse or press Enter to anchor the pane line. Word replaces the thick, transparent line with a second ruler for the new document pane.

Removing Window Panes

To remove a window pane, choose the Window menu's Remove Split command. (This command replaces Split on this menu after you've split a window into panes.)

Jumping between window panes

You can move the **insertion point** between window panes by clicking.

Wizards

If you want to create a complicated document— a newsletter or a legal pleading, for example—Word provides a special tool you may find useful. When you choose the File menu's New command to create a new document, you can select one of the wizards identified on one of the tabs. When you do, Word collects information about the document you want to create and uses this data to make a series of **document, section,** and **paragraph** formatting decisions. You may never need to use this feature, but take a look at the **templates** that appear on the tabs of the New dialog box. You can probably save yourself some time by doing so.

WordArt

Microsoft Word comes with a supplementary **program** named WordArt that lets you manipulate text in all sorts of unusual ways. When you use WordArt, you're embedding WordArt **objects** in a document.

Starting WordArt

To start WordArt, choose the Insert menu's Picture command and then choose the submenu's WordArt command. The figure that follows shows an example document with text manipulated by using WordArt.

Here is an example of text manipulated with Word Art.

continues

WordArt *(continued)*

Creating a WordArt Object

After you've started WordArt, you'll see the WordArt Gallery. Click the style you want, and then click OK.

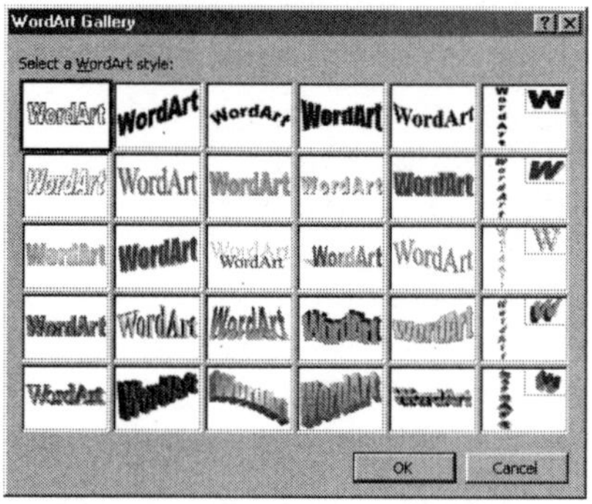

When WordArt displays the Edit WordArt Text dialog box, enter the text you want to manipulate. Then click OK, and Word inserts the WordArt object in your document.

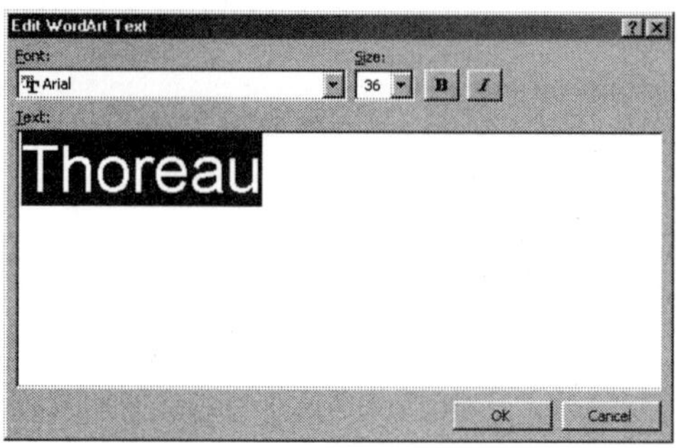

Formatting the WordArt Object Text

You can use the WordArt toolbar buttons to manipulate the text you've entered. The following table describes each of these tools:

Tool	What it does
	Displays the WordArt Gallery for you to add more WordArt.
Edit Text...	Displays your WordArt text in the Edit WordArt Text window, where you can change text, font, and point size.
	Displays the WordArt Gallery for you to change the style of the selected WordArt object.
	Displays the Format WordArt dialog box with tabs for modifying color and lines, size, position, and wrapping for your WordArt object.
	Displays a gallery of shapes that can be applied to the WordArt text.
	Rotates WordArt text.
	Displays a submenu of options for wrapping text around your WordArt object.
	Makes all letters the same height or undoes the same height.
	Switches between vertical and horizontal text.
	Displays a menu of WordArt alignment styles.
	Displays a menu where you can modify the spacing between WordArt letters.

Word Count

You can easily count the number of pages, words, **characters, paragraphs,** and lines in a **document.** To do so, first be sure that the document is active, and then choose the Tools menu's Word Count command. Word displays the Word Count dialog box, and after a few milliseconds of counting, shows the document's statistics.

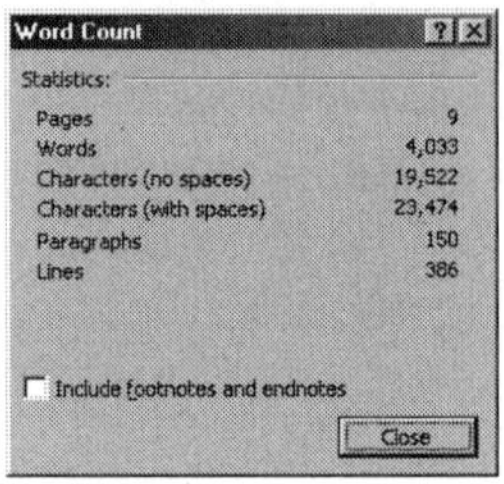

WordPerfect

WordPerfect is another very popular word-processing application. Because many, many people use WordPerfect, you should know that it's possible to both export Word documents to WordPerfect and import WordPerfect documents into Word.

Moving a Document from Word to WordPerfect

To move a document from Word to WordPerfect, choose the File menu's Save As command. Complete the dialog box in the usual way, and also specify the file type as the appropriate WordPerfect file. To do this, select a file type from the Save As Type drop-down list box.

Moving a Document from WordPerfect to Word

To move a document from WordPerfect to Word, first save the document in WordPerfect. Then start Word, and choose the File menu's Open command. Complete the dialog box in the usual way, and also specify the file type as one of the WordPerfect file formats. To do this, select a file type from the Files Of Type drop-down list box.

SEE ALSO Exporting Documents; Importing Documents

Word Wrap

Word wrap just means that Word moves the **insertion point** to the next line as soon as you run out of room on the current line. Word will also move big words to the next line if the move makes things fit better. Although word wrap is a simple little feature, it's one of the big reasons that word processors such as Word are much, much easier to use than typewriters.

SEE ALSO Nonbreaking Spaces

World Wide Web

The World Wide Web (also known as WWW or simply the Web) is a set of multimedia documents that are connected so that you can jump from one document to another by using **hyperlinks,** usually with just a mouse click. The multimedia part means that you're not limited to words; you can place pictures, sounds, and even video clips in a web document.

To view a web page, you need to have an Internet service provider (like America Online, The Microsoft Network, or one of the local Internet providers in your area). You also need a **web browser.** Some popular web browsers are Netscape Navigator, and Microsoft Internet Explorer. If you want to start exploring the Web, see the entry for **Microsoft on the Web** and choose the Search The Web menu item.

SEE ALSO HTML; URL; Web Page

Zooming

You can both magnify and reduce (or shrink) the characters shown on your screen. You can either choose the View menu's Zoom command or click the Zoom toolbar button.

continues

Zooming *(continued)*

Magnifying

Click the down arrow on the Zoom toolbar button, or choose the View menu's Zoom command. Then select a percentage. Selecting 200%, for example, magnifies everything to twice its actual size. You can also type a larger size percentage in the Zoom box.

Shrinking

Click the down arrow on the Zoom toolbar button, or choose the View menu's Zoom command. Then select a percentage. Selecting 50%, for example, reduces everything to half its actual size. You can also type a smaller size percentage in the Zoom box.

Zooming doesn't affect printing

When you zoom a document, you don't change the character point size. You merely magnify or shrink the display. As a result, zooming doesn't change what your printed document looks like. To do that, choose the Format menu's Font command.

Troubleshooting

Got a problem? Starting on the next page are solutions to the problems that sometimes plague new users of Microsoft Word 2000. You'll be on your way—and safely out of trouble—in no time.

Tables

You Can't Get Table Gridlines to Print

Word displays table gridlines to make it easier for you to see a table's columns and rows. The gridlines, therefore, are for display purposes only. They don't print. If you want to print lines to show a table's rows and columns, you'll need to add borders.

AutoFormat a table

This technique is the easiest way to add border lines.

1. Select the table.
2. Choose the Table menu's Table AutoFormat command.
3. When Word displays the Table AutoFormat dialog box, select a table style in the Formats box.

Add a border grid

You can also add border lines manually.

1. Select the table.
2. Choose the Format menu's Borders And Shading command.
3. Click the Borders tab.
4. Click either the Grid or the All option button under Setting.

SEE ALSO **Paragraphs; Table Borders**

You Can't Get a Table Formula to Calculate

The **formulas** you enter in table cells aren't updated automatically. You need to tell Word when it's time to recalculate.

Manually force recalculation

To tell Word that it should recalculate a formula, click the formula and press F9.

You Can't Correctly Calculate a Table Formula

Even if formula results seem wrong, Word is calculating the formula correctly. The problem is that the formula you've entered isn't actually the one you want to calculate. Your problem boils down to one of operator precedence.

Override the standard operator precedence

To force Word to calculate in the order you want, enclose in parentheses the first calculation you want performed. Then enclose in parentheses the second calculation you want performed. Then enclose the third calculation, and so on.

Menus and Toolbars

Your Menu Commands Disappear

Word has a new feature: Personal Menus. When you first start working with the program, it keeps track of those menu commands you use and don't use and automatically customizes your menus. It's a cool feature; because the menu's shorter, it's easier to access the commands you use most.

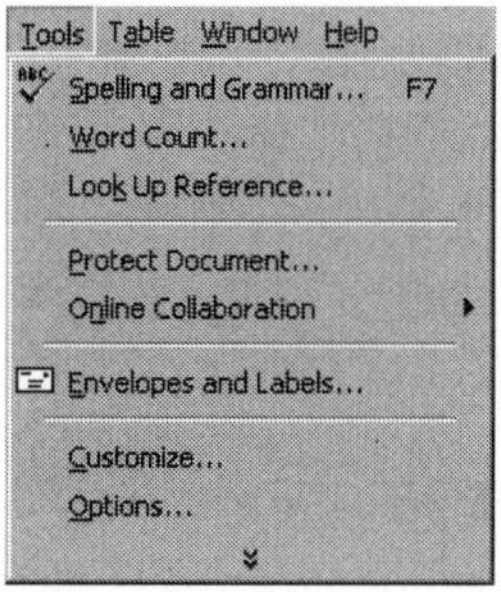

However, it can be a little disconcerting when commands just up and vanish.

Find the missing commands

The hidden commands aren't really gone; they're just hiding. To use one of them, just hold your cursor on the menu title for a few seconds, and the full list of commands will pop up.

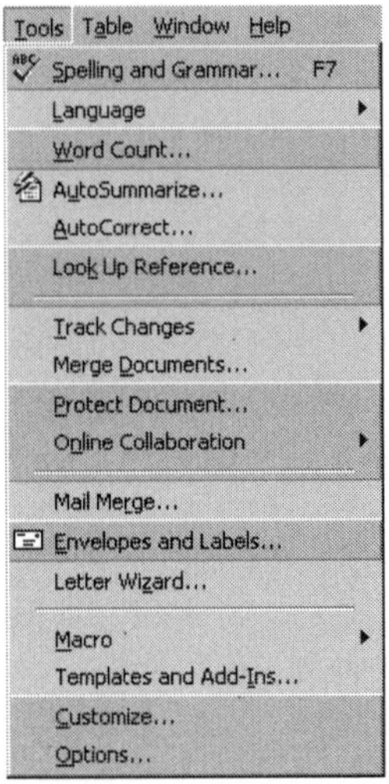

If the list doesn't pop up, choose the Tools menu's Customize command, click the Options tab, and make sure that the Show Full Menus After A Short Delay check box is selected.

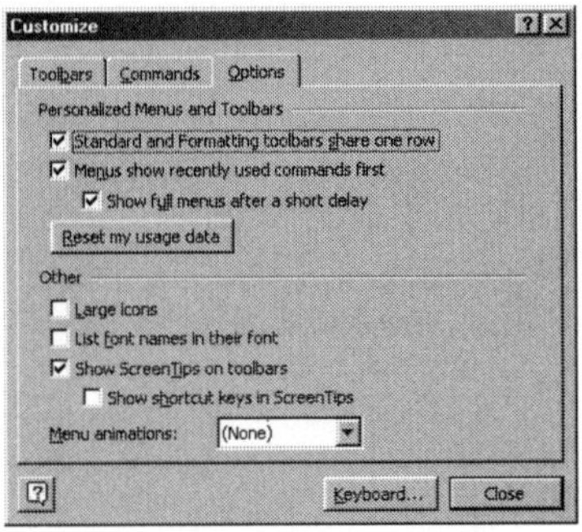

Reset your menus and toolbars

You can also reset your menus and toolbars to their original configuration by clicking Reset My Usage Data. Word will start learning your preferences all over again.

Your Toolbar Buttons Appear or Disappear

Along with Personal Menus, Word has Personal Toolbars. The program customizes your toolbar to display the buttons you use most.

Find your missing buttons

Click the little double-chevron button on the Personal toolbar.

Your missing buttons will pop up in a toolbar extension.

Customize the toolbar manually

If you want to manually control what's on your toolbar, you can click either Add or Remove Buttons on the toolbar extension, or choose the Tools menu's Customize command, click the Commands tab, and drag and drop buttons to and from the toolbars to suit your needs.

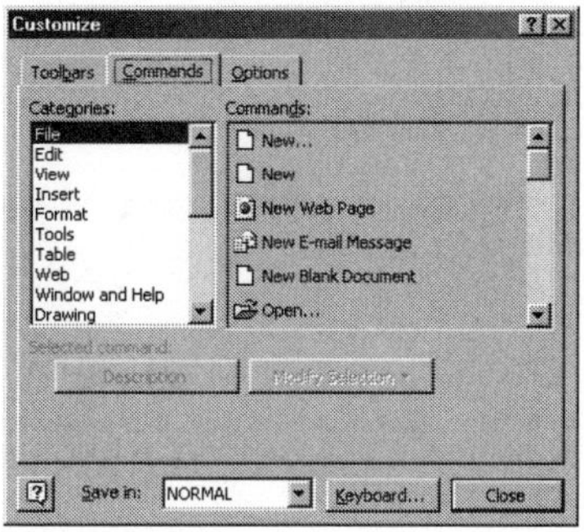

Printing

You Want to Stop Page Breaking

Often Word will break a document across pages—even though you don't want it to. It breaks pages because it has run out of room on a page. You can change where Word breaks pages by increasing the page space available for printing and by condensing page information.

Change the page dimensions

One of the easier ways you can stop or minimize a document's page breaking is to reduce the margins. Reducing the left and right margins makes lines of text longer, of course, and reducing the top and bottom margins allows more lines on a page. Smaller page margins, therefore, increase the size of the printable page area.

To reduce the page margins, choose the File menu's Page Setup command, click the Margins tab, and change the margin settings.

Reduce the font size

Another way to pack more information on a page is to use a smaller **point** size. You can do that by entering a smaller number in the Font Size box.

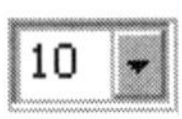

Another approach is to use a narrower font—such as a condensed font. To get even more text on a page, use a proportional font, such as Times Roman. Change your font in the Font box.

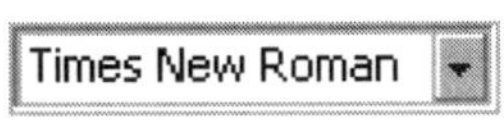

Previewing pages

To see what your printed pages will look like, click the Print Preview toolbar button. You can also choose the View menu's Print Layout command.

You Want to Cancel a Printing Document

If you've told Word that you want it to print a **document** you later realize you don't need or want, you can cancel the printing of the document, particularly if the document is large or your printer is slow.

Cancel printing from within Word

When Word is printing a document, it displays a printing indicator on the status bar. The indicator features a little animated printer symbol.

If you double-click the printing indicator, Word cancels the printing.

Cancel printing by using Windows

If the printing indicator is gone, Word has finished sending the print spool file to Windows. (Windows prints this print spool file as well as any other spool files that Word and other programs have sent.) To cancel printing at this point, you need to follow these steps:

1 Click the Start button. Choose Settings, and then choose Printers to display the Printers window.

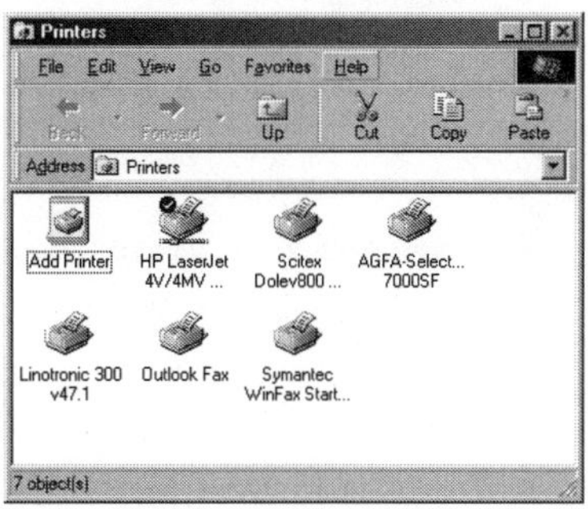

2 Double-click the printer icon for the printer you're using to display the print queue for the printer.

continues

You Want to Cancel a Printing Document *(continued)*

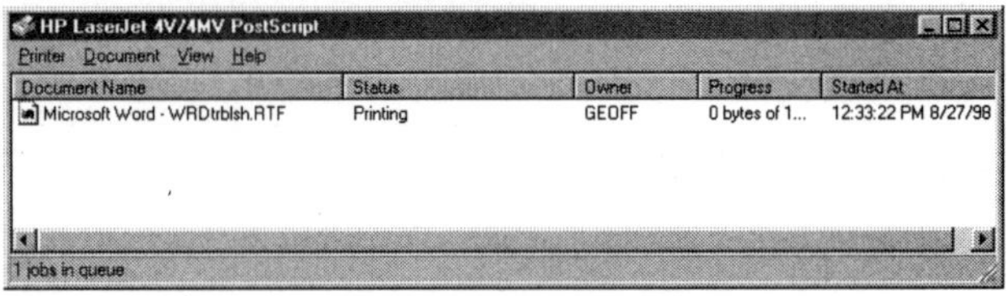

3 Click the Word document that's being printed.

4 Press Delete, or choose the Document menu's Cancel Printing command.

SEE ALSO **Printing; Switching Tasks; Window Buttons**

Display

You Can't See the Menu

If you choose Full Screen from the View menu, Word displays only the document. It doesn't show the **program window** title bar, the menu bar, or the **toolbars.** If you aren't familiar with Full Screen view, it can be a bit confusing.

Click the Full Screen button

If you or someone else has just switched to Full Screen view, Word displays a Full Screen button. Click Close Full Screen to return to the regular screen view (Normal view). You can also press the Esc key.

Choose the Full Screen command

If someone has removed the Full Screen button by clicking its Close button, you obviously can't use the button to return to Normal view. Move the mouse pointer to the top of the screen. When you do, Word displays the menu bar. Choose the View menu's Full Screen command.

You Can't See Graphics on the Screen or They Don't Print

If you don't see the graphics images or drawn objects you've added or they don't print, your problem may be solved in any of three ways.

Turn off Draft Output

Word's Draft Output option prints a document without character formatting or graphics. To turn off the Draft Output option, follow these steps:

1. Choose the Tools menu's Options command.
2. Click the Print tab.
3. Select the Draft Output check box to clear it.

Turn on Drawing Objects

If drawn objects are the only ones that aren't printing, someone may have turned off Word's Drawing Objects option. To get this ball rolling again, follow these steps:

1. Choose the Tools menu's Options command.
2. Click the Print tab.
3. Select the Drawing Objects check box if it isn't already selected.

Drawn objects won't display

If drawn objects aren't displayed, follow these steps:

1. Choose the Tools menu's Options command.
2. Click the View tab.
3. Select the Picture Placeholders check box to clear it.

Free up some memory

One other potential problem: Word may not have enough memory to draw and display things like drawn objects. You can address this problem by closing inactive Word **documents.**

Another thing you can do is switch to any of your other open programs and close them.

SEE ALSO Control Menu Commands; Switching Tasks

Files

You Can't Save a Document

Word needs a certain amount of system "horsepower"—principally memory—to save a **document.** If your available system resources get too low, you can run into some serious problems. Fortunately, as long as you keep your cool, this situation doesn't have to be a disaster. Your basic approach is a simple one. You want to free up system resources and then try resaving the document.

Close your other open programs

Switch to any of your other open programs and close them. You can switch to the other open programs by clicking their buttons on the Taskbar; or, if your Taskbar isn't on top or visible, press Alt+Tab to activate the other programs' windows, and then choose the File menu's Exit command.

After you've closed all the other programs (and saved their documents, if that's appropriate), return to Word and try resaving the document you couldn't save earlier.

Try opening another session of Word or WordPad

Sometimes you'll close all the other open Windows programs and still can't save the document. This situation may happen because even though you've freed up system resources, Word can't use those resources. A newly started program, however, may be able to use the resources. To save the document, follow these steps:

1. Start WordPad or a second copy of Word. (Refer to the **Switching Tasks** entry if that's not something you know how to do.)
2. Copy the unsavable document to the Clipboard by selecting the entire document (the easiest way is to press Ctrl+A) and clicking the Copy toolbar button (or choosing the Edit menu's Copy command).
3. Switch to the newly started program by clicking its button on the Taskbar.
4. Paste the Clipboard contents in the new document by choosing the Edit menu's Paste command.
5. Save the new document by using a new filename.

SEE ALSO **Saving Documents**

You Can't Find a Document

A lost document doesn't have to be as big a problem as you think, because Windows provides an extremely powerful tool for finding lost files: the Find File program.

Use the Find File program

To start Find File, click the Start button, choose Find, and then choose Files Or Folders. Windows displays the Find: All Files dialog box.

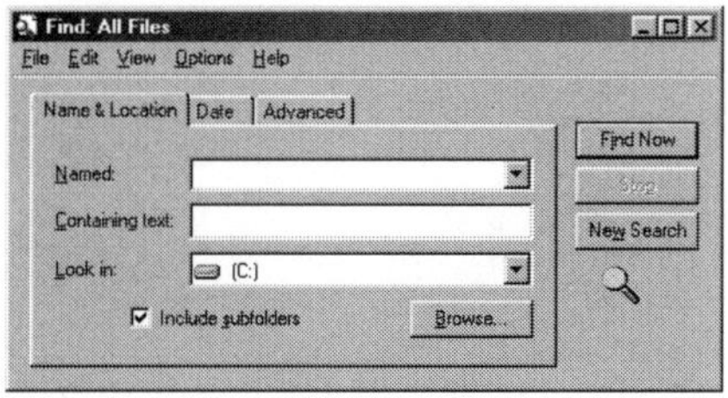

1. If you know the filename, enter it in the Named box. You can use wildcard characters as part of the filename.
2. Select a location from the Look In drop-down list box to tell Windows where to look.
3. Select the Include Subfolders check box if you want to look in both folders and subfolders.
4. To describe the last modification date of the file, click the Date tab.

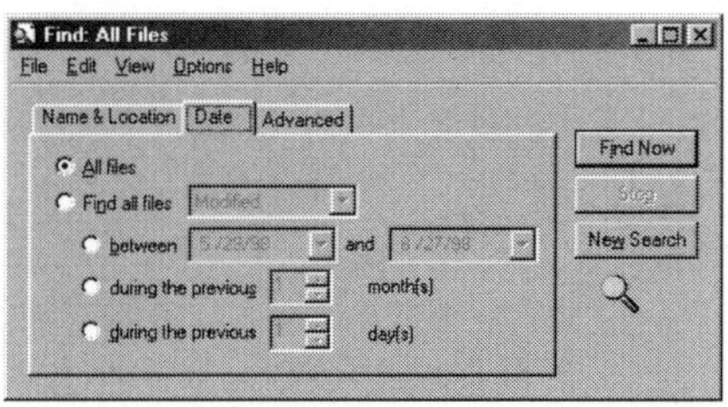

5. Or use the Advanced tab's options to describe some string of text in the file or the file size.

continues

You Can't Find a Document *(continued)*

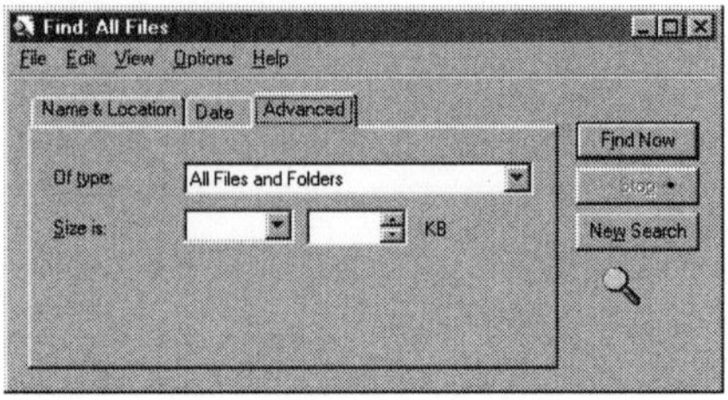

6 Click Find Now to start the search. Windows displays the Find: All Files window with a list of the files.

You Accidentally Erased a Document

If you erase or delete a file and later realize that you shouldn't have, all is not lost. The Recycle Bin stores deleted files. (Note that when the Recycle Bin eventually does fill up, Microsoft Windows makes room for new deleted files in the Recycle Bin by removing the oldest deleted files. So you can't undelete really old files by using the Recycle Bin.)

Restore the file

To restore a file you've deleted, follow these steps:

1 Double-click the Recycle Bin icon to display the Recycle Bin window.

2 Select the file you want to restore.

3 Choose the File menu's Restore command.

SEE ALSO **Opening Documents; Saving Documents**

You Can't Remember Your Password

If you or someone else assigned a read reservation password to a document file, you'll need to supply that password before you open the file. If you forget your password or can't seem to enter it correctly, Word won't let you open the document.

Try a password with different-case letters

Word differentiates passwords on the basis of the letter-case. The following words, for example, are all different passwords from Word's point of view: Wathers, wATHERS, and WATHERS. For this reason, if you think that you know the password, try changing the lowercase letters to uppercase letters and vice versa. You may have entered the password with a different combination of uppercase and lowercase letters than you think (for instance, if you happen to press the Caps Lock key before entering the password).

SEE ALSO **Opening Documents; Save Options; Saving Documents**

Windows and Programs

Word Gives You an Error Message or Behaves Oddly

Word is a large, complex program. Sometimes files get corrupted, which can adversely affect performance.

Run Detect And Repair

Choose the Help menu's Detect And Repair command to fix noncritical files, such as font files.

You Can't Get Word to Respond

It's unlikely but still possible that a bug in Word or in some other program will cause the program to stop responding. If this happens, you won't be able to choose menu commands, and you may not be able to move the mouse pointer.

Terminate the unresponsive program

Unfortunately, if a program is truly unresponsive—if it ignores your keyboard and mouse actions—you can't do anything to make it start responding again.

In this case, press Ctrl+Alt+Del. (You press the three keys simultaneously.) This key combination tells Windows to look at all programs and check them for responsiveness. Windows then displays the Close Program dialog box, identifying any unresponsive program as "not responding."

continues

You Can't Get Word to Respond *(continued)*

To terminate a program, select it, and then click End Task. To shut down or reboot your computer, click Shut Down. To close the Close Program dialog box without doing anything, click Close.

Before you conclude that Word or some other program is ignoring you, consider the possibility that it's busy working. If the hard disk light is flickering, something is happening! Word, for example, may be running a macro. Another program may be creating a print spool file or executing another command you've given it.

Terminating programs with Windows NT

The preceding discussion explains how to terminate an unresponsive program with Windows 95 or 98. With Windows NT and Windows 2000, the steps work differently. Press Ctrl+Alt+Del, click Task Manager, select the unresponsive program, and then click End Task.

You Get a Program Error

Sometimes a program asks Windows to do the impossible. When this happens—which isn't very often—Windows displays a message box that says a program error has occurred.

Close the program

When Windows does alert you to an program error, it usually gives you two choices: Close and Details. You want to select Close.

In rare cases, Windows might give you the option of ignoring the error. Even in this case, the most prudent choice is still to close the program.

By the way, if you've been working with a **document,** have made changes you haven't yet saved, and have the option of ignoring the error, you should ignore the program error and then save the document. Do save the document by using a new **filename,** however. You don't want to replace the previous version of the document with a new, possibly corrupted, version. After you've saved the document, close the program.

Quick Reference

Any time you explore a new program, you're bound to see features and tools you can't identify. To be sure you can identify the commands and toolbar buttons you see in Microsoft Word 2000, this Quick Reference describes these items in systematic detail.

Word Menu Guide

File Menu

New...	Opens a new, blank document based on the document template you select or allows you to create a new document template.
Open...	Retrieves an existing document.
Close	Removes the active document's window from the screen.
Save	Resaves the active document as long as you've already saved it at least once.
Save As...	Saves a document the first time or with a new name.
Save As Web Page...	Saves a document as an HTML document you can publish on an Internet web site.
Versions...	Displays existing versions of the open document, with options to save new versions or view comments in any version.
Web Page Preview	Displays a window showing how the document will look as web pages.
Page Setup...	Allows you to set page size, orientation, margins, and other layout options.
Print Preview	Displays a window showing how printed document pages will look.
Print...	Prints the active document.
Send To	Displays the Send To submenu.

Mail Recipient...	Sends the current Word document in an e-mail message to the recipient(s) you choose.
Mail Recipient (As Attachment)...	Sends the current Word document to the recipient(s) you choose, as an attachment to an e-mail message.
Routing Recipient...	Sends the current Word document to a group of e-mail recipients and allows you to specify whether it is sent to them sequentially or all at one time.

Exchange Folder...	Sends the current Word document to a folder in your Exchange client mailbox or to a Public folder where it can be read by others.
Online Meeting Participant	Sends the current document to one or more persons in a NetMeeting conference.
Fax Recipient...	Starts the Fax Wizard to help you send your Word document as a fax.
Microsoft PowerPoint	Sends the current Word document to Microsoft PowerPoint.

Properties	Displays information about the active document.
Exit	Closes, or shuts down, Word.

Numbered File menu commands

Word also lists as File menu commands the last four documents you saved. You can open a listed document by choosing it from the File menu.

Edit Menu

Undo	Reverses, or undoes, the last document change.
Repeat	Duplicates the last document change.
Cut	Moves the current document selection to the Clipboard.
Copy	Moves a copy of the current document selection to the Clipboard.
Paste	Copies the Clipboard contents to the active document.
Paste Special...	Copies some portion of the Clipboard contents to the active document.
Paste As Hyperlink	Copies into the document a field that lets you jump to another location.
Clear	Erases the current selection.
Select All	Selects the entire document.

continues

Edit Menu *(continued)*

Find...	Looks for text or formatting that matches a specified description.
Replace...	Looks for text or formatting that matches a specified description and (optionally) replaces it.
Go To...	Moves the insertion point to a specified location.
Links...	Describes, updates, and changes the selected object's link.
Object	Opens the selected object so that it can be modified or allows you to convert the object into another form.

View Menu

Normal	Displays the document as a single column of text.
Web Layout	Displays the document as it will look as a web page.
Page Layout	Displays the document as laid-out pages.
Outline	Displays the document in outline form.
Toolbars	Lets you specify which toolbars will appear on your screen.
Ruler	Turns on and off the ruler display at the top of the page.
Document Map	Turns on and off a pane in the document window that outlines the document's structure.
Header And Footer	Opens the header and footer editing areas on laid-out pages.
Footnotes	Opens the Footnote pane at the bottom of the document window.
Comments	Opens the Comment pane at the bottom of the document window.
Full Screen	Displays only the document window and hides all menus and toolbars.
Zoom...	Magnifies and reduces the on-screen document by a specified percentage.

Insert Menu

Break...	Breaks the column, page, or section at the insertion point.
Page Numbers...	Numbers the pages of a document.

Date And Time...	Places the current date or time at the insertion point.
AutoText	Lets you create and enter various AutoText entries, such as salutations and signature lines.
Field...	Places a field code at the insertion point.
Symbol...	Adds a symbol at the insertion point.
Comment	Opens the Comment pane at the bottom of the page so that you can add commentary.
Footnote...	Places a footnote or endnote at the insertion point and opens the Footnote or Endnote pane.
Caption...	Places a figure caption above or below the selected object.
Cross-Reference...	Adds a cross-reference entry for the selected term.
Index And Tables...	Adds an index, table of contents, table of figures, or table of authorities at the insertion point.
Picture	Displays the Picture submenu.
	Clip Art... Displays the Microsoft Clip Art Gallery dialog box so that you can add clip art images to the document.
	From File... Displays the Insert Picture dialog box so that you can insert a picture from a file on a disk.
	AutoShapes Displays the AutoShapes toolbar so that you can add shapes and symbols to your document.
	WordArt... Displays the WordArt Gallery dialog box so that you can add WordArt to your document.
	From Scanner Or Camera Opens the Microsoft Photo Editor application so that you can add scanned or digital photo images to your worksheets.
	Chart Starts Microsoft Graph so that you can insert a chart into your document.
Text Box	Adds a text box object to the document.
File...	Inserts another document file's contents into the open document at the insertion point.
Object...	Embeds or links another application's object in or to the document.

continues

Insert Menu *(continued)*

Bookmark...	Inserts and sorts bookmarks.
Hyperlink...	Adds a link to another file or URL.

Format Menu

Font...	Changes the font and spacing of selected characters.
Paragraph...	Changes the indentation, alignment, and numbering of the selected paragraph.
Bullets And Numbering...	Adds and formats bullets or numbers to the selected paragraphs.
Borders And Shading...	Changes the borders and shading for the selected paragraph, table, or picture.
Columns...	Changes the number of columns used in a document section.
Tabs...	Sets and clears tab stops for the selected paragraph.
Drop Cap...	Creates dropped capital letters.
Text Direction...	Changes the orientation of text in a text frame.
Change Case...	Changes the case (upper vs. lower) of the selected letters.
Background...	Changes the color of a document's background for screen display and printing on color-capable printers.
Theme...	Applies a complete set of styles, including custom backgrounds, to a document.
Frames	Inserts frames for building web pages.
AutoFormat...	Automatically applies formatting, including font and paragraph formats, to the current document.
Style...	Lets you apply and create styles.
Object	Formats the selected object.

Tools Menu

Spelling And Grammar...	Checks the spelling and grammar of the current document or selection.	
Language	Displays the Language submenu.	
	Set Language...	Lets you specify which language dictionary should be used for checking spelling in the current document or selection.
	Thesaurus...	Shows synonyms for the selected word.
	Hyphenation...	Lets you specify how Word should hyphenate words.
Word Count...	Counts the pages, words, characters, paragraphs, and lines in a document.	
AutoSummarize...	Automatically summarizes the key points in a document.	
AutoCorrect...	Lets you determine which automatic typing corrections Word should make.	
Look Up Reference...	Researches keywords in available reference resources.	
Track Changes	Displays the Track Changes submenu.	
	Highlight Changes...	Tracks changes and highlights them on screen or on the printed page.
	Accept Or Reject Changes...	Finds tracked changes so that you can review them and then accept, reject, or ignore them.
	Compare Documents...	Compares the open document with the original document and marks the changes.
Merge Documents...	Merges other files into the open document.	
Protect Document...	Protects a document by limiting changes.	
Online Collaboration	Displays the Online Collaboration submenu.	
	Meet Now	Begins a NetMeeting session.
	Schedule Meeting...	Uses Microsoft Outlook to schedule a NetMeeting.
	Web Discussions	Begins a web discussion session.

continues

Tools Menu *(continued)*

Mail Merge...	Generates form letters, labels, envelopes, and catalogs.
Envelopes And Labels...	Prints envelopes and labels.
Letter Wizard...	Automates practically everything about writing a letter.
Macro	Displays the Macro submenu.

	Macros	Runs a macro.
	Record New Macro	Adds a macro sheet so that you can record a macro.
	Security	Controls the screening of macros for viruses.
	Visual Basic Editor	Creates a Visual Basic macro.
	Microsoft Script Editor	Writes or edits VBScript or JavaScript.

Templates And Add-Ins...	Shows which template is attached to the open document and lets you use styles from other templates and add-ins.
Customize...	Customizes the Word toolbars, menus, and shortcut keys
Options...	Controls Word's operation with a dialog box packed with ten pages of options.

Table Menu

Draw Table	Draws a table in the document.
Insert	Displays the Insert submenu.

	Table...	Adds a table to a document.
	Columns To The Left	Adds column(s) to the left of selected cells in an existing table.
	Columns To The Right	Adds column(s) to the right of selected cells in an existing table.
	Rows Above	Adds row(s) above selected cells in an existing table.

	Rows Below	Adds row(s) below selected cells in an existing table.
	Cells	Adds individual cells to an existing table.
Delete	Displays the Delete submenu.	
	Table	Deletes entire selected table.
	Columns	Deletes selected column(s) from a table.
	Rows	Deletes selected row(s) from a table.
	Cells	Deletes selected cell(s) from a table.
Select	Displays the Select submenu.	
	Table	Selects entire table.
	Columns	Selects one or more columns from a table.
	Rows	Selects one or more rows from a table.
	Cells	Selects one or more cells from a table.
Merge Cells	Combines selected cells into one.	
Split Cells...	Splits one cell into two or more.	
Split Table...	Splits a table above the selected row by inserting a paragraph.	
Table AutoFormat...	Formats the selected table automatically, including font and borders.	
AutoFit	Displays the AutoFit submenu.	
	AutoFit To Contents	Adjusts to fit text within column widths.
	Autofit To Window	Adjusts column widths to fit window.
	Fixed Column Width	Creates fixed column widths.
	Distribute Rows Evenly	Spaces selected rows evenly within the table.
	Distribute Columns Evenly	Spaces selected columns evenly within the table.

continues

Table Menu *(continued)*

Heading Rows Repeat...	Tells Word to print table heading rows on each page on which the table appears.
Convert	Displays the Convert submenu.
	Text To Table... Turns regular text into tables.
	Table To Text... Turns tables into regular text.
Sort...	Arranges the order of the selected table rows or the selected paragraphs.
Formula...	Adds a formula to the selected cell.
Hide Gridlines...	Turns the display of table gridlines on and off.
Table Properties...	Controls height, width, and alignment of tables, rows, columns, and cells.

Window Menu

New Window	Opens a new window for the active document.
Arrange All	Displays all the open document windows in tiles.
Split/Remove Split	Splits or unsplits the active document window.

Your commands are numbered

Word also lists all the open document windows as numbered Window menu commands. You can open a listed window by choosing it from the Window menu.

Help Menu

Microsoft Word Help	Starts the Office Assistant or opens the Help System.
Hide/Show The Office Assistant	Hides the Office Assistant character or shows it, if it's hidden.
What's This?	Displays helpful information about whatever you click next: a menu command, a toolbar button, or an element of the Word application or document window.

Office On The Web Connects you to a variety of Microsoft forums on the World Wide Web to get help with your questions.

WordPerfect Help... Indicates how to accomplish a WordPerfect task in Word.

Detect And Repair... Automatically find and fix problems with Word.

About Microsoft Word Displays the copyright notice, the software version number, and your computer's available memory.

Toolbar Guide

Standard Toolbar

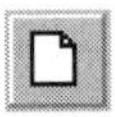 Creates a new, blank document.

 Opens an existing document.

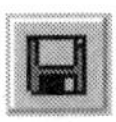 Saves the active document on disk.

 E-mails the current document.

 Prints the active document.

 Shows what the printed pages of a document will look like.

Checks spelling and grammar in the active document.

 Moves the current document selection to the Clipboard.

 Moves a copy of the current document selection to the Clipboard.

 Copies the Clipboard contents to the active document.

 Copies the formatting of the current document selection to the next document selection.

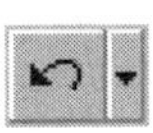 Undoes the last document change.

Standard Toolbar *(continued)*

Button	Description
	Repeats the last action that was undone.
	Inserts a hyperlink field into the active document.
	Displays the Tables and Borders toolbar and draws a table in your document.
	Inserts an empty table at the insertion point.
	Inserts a blank Microsoft Excel worksheet at the insertion point.
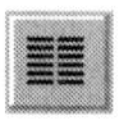	Changes the number of text columns per page.
	Activates the Drawing tool.
	Turns on and off a pane in the window that outlines the document's structure.
	Shows and hides nonprinting characters.
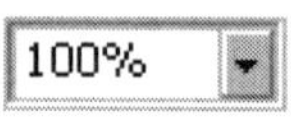	Magnifies or reduces document contents by the specified zoom percentage.
	Turns on the Office Assistant for help topics and tips.

Formatting Toolbar

Button	Description
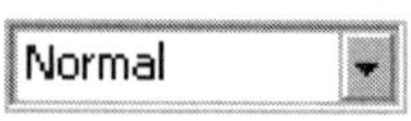	Changes the style of the selected text.
	Changes the font of the selected text.
	Changes the point size of the selected text.
	Bolds the characters in the selected text.
	Italicizes the characters in the selected text.

Underlines the characters in the selected text.

Left-aligns the selected paragraphs.

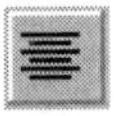
Centers the selected paragraphs.

Right-aligns the selected paragraphs.

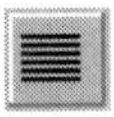
Justifies the selected paragraphs.

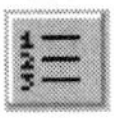
Numbers the selected paragraphs.

Adds bullets to each of the selected paragraphs.

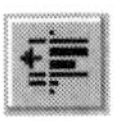
Moves the left paragraph margin to the left.

Moves the left paragraph margin to the right.

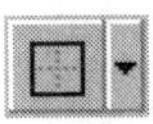
Displays the Borders toolbar.

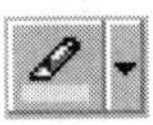
Highlights text by coloring it.

Changes the color of the selected text.

Drawing Toolbar

Displays the drawing menu.

Selects drawn objects.

Rotates drawn objects on the page.

Displays a gallery of shapes for adding or modifying drawn objects.

continues

Drawing Toolbar *(continued)*

Button	Description
	Draws a straight line.
	Draws an arrow.
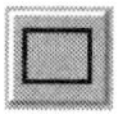	Draws rectangles and squares.
	Draws ellipses and circles.
	Adds a text box.
	Adds a WordArt object.
	Inserts clip art.
	Fills objects with color.
	Controls line color.
	Colors the fonts used in drawn objects.
	Changes the line thickness and style.
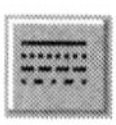	Changes the dash style.
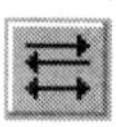	Changes arrow styles.
	Adds shading and shadows to a drawn object.
	Adds three-dimensional effects to a drawn object.

Web Toolbar

Jumps backward to the previous web page.

Jumps forward to the next web page.

Cancels a jump.

Redisplays the current web page.

Jumps to the web page you've specified as your start page.

Opens a search page on the Web.

Displays a menu of your own personal favorite web sites.

Displays a menu of web commands like those on the toolbar and also includes options to define your start and search pages.

Removes from the screen all toolbars except the Web toolbar.

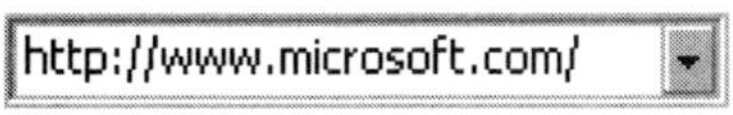

Displays current web page address or document path.

A

B

C

D

E

N

O

P

R

S

T

U

V

W